Phonics is Fun

Teacher's Manual

Grade 2

By Louis Krane, Ed. D.

Reprinted and electronically reproduced by permission of Pearson Education, Inc., New York, NY.

Copyright ©2017, 2021 by St. Jerome Library Press

Original copyright 1990 by Pearson Education, Inc., publishing as Modern Curriculum Press

St. Jerome Library

WWW.STJEROMELIBRARY.ORG

Phonics Is Fun

Faster-paced instruction for more capable students.
Now, from MCP, a phonics program that maximizes students' ability to learn as it minimizes teacher-preparation time.

Complete, systematic phonics instruction

Phonics Is Fun provides instruction in the minimum number of phonetic skills which will assure word recognition. The sequence of these essential skills is based on the frequency with which phonetic elements occur in the English language. Thus, the scope and sequence of skills is designed to provide students with a viable set of phonetic word-attack skills, enabling them to read an unlimited number of words.

More capable students quickly take responsibility for their own learning

The instruction is accomplished through a multi-sensory approach, using auditory and visual discrimination exercises, sound blending, and word pronunciation, and culminating in reading, spelling, and writing words in sentences. The students are presented with the minimum number of rules and definitions for achieving reading independence. The students quickly develop the ability to relate the printed word to its speech equivalent and comprehend the meaning of words in context.

All new, contemporary artwork

The attractive, clear artwork will hold students' interest as they work through the pages. The picture cues provide for vocabulary development, but since they are easy to identify, they never interfere with the learning of the phonetic skills.

New, expanded Teacher's Edition

This Teacher's Edition maximizes your teaching efforts as it minimizes the amount of preparation time. There is an array of completely described games and activities for multisensory practice of phonetic skills. These games and activities only require common, easily found materials. The pictures are clearly labeled and the answers easily readable. Blackline masters provide for skills assessment, and family involvement activities enable you to keep parents informed of their children's progress.

Student Edition with instruction that moves at a faster, more challenging pace.

More items per page, providing more concentrated practice.

Faster, more challenging pace of instruction.

Variety of formats to hold students' attention.

All-new, interest-capturing artwork.

Students master the minimum number of important phonetic skills, applying them in meaningful contexts.

Teacher's Edition that maximizes your time.

Review automatically builds in maintenance of previously-learned phonetic skills.

Teaching Ideas describes games and activities that provide multisensory involvement through listening, speaking, reading and writing.

Reteaching suggests activities for helping students who didn't master the skill the first time through.

Extension challenges students who have been successful.

Blackline masters for assessment.

Family Involvement activities that are cross-referenced with reproducible letters to parents.

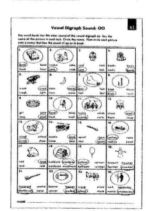

Scope and Sequence for Phonics Is Fun

Lesson Numbers

Skill	Book 1	Book 2	Book 3
Visual Discrimination	1		
Recognition of Letters	2–7	1	1
Consonant Letter-Sound Associations	8–27	2–10	2–4
Short Vowels: *A*	28–30	11	5
I	31–33	12	6
U	34–36	13	7
O	37–39	14	8
E	40–42	15	9
Long Vowels: *A*	43–45	18	11
I	46–48	19	11
U	49–51	20	12
O	52–54	21	12
E	55–57	22	13
Review of Vowels 58			
Suffixes	59–61	36–45	39–44, 57
Consonant Blends: *R* Blends	62	24	15
L Blends	63	25	16
S Blends	64	26	17
Y as a Vowel	65	27	20
Consonant Digraphs	66–68	29, 30, 58, 59	18, 19, 34, 35
Compound Words	16, 23	10,14	
Two-Syllable Words		17, 23	10
W as a Vowel		28	20
Hard and Soft *C* and *G*		31, 32	21–23
Vowels with *R*		33–35	24–26
Contractions		46–49	58
Vowel Digraphs	50–53	27–30	
Kn		58	35
Wr		59	35
Ending *Le*		60	36
Prefixes		61	46–49
Synonyms		62	59
Antonyms		63	60
Homonyms		64	61
Diphthongs		54–57	31–33
Syllabication			37, 38, 45, 50–56

To the Teacher

The *Phonics Is Fun* program consists of a phonetic-semantic approach to word recognition. Characterized by strong auditory training, the program presents a minimum of rules, definitions, and variations of consonant and vowel sounds. In *Phonics Is Fun*, the child quickly develops the ability to associate letters and sounds, relate the printed word to its speech equivalent, and comprehend the meaning of words in context. The program increases the child's reading vocabulary to correspond with the verbal and auditory vocabulary. *Phonics Is Fun* is designed to provide the child with a viable set of phonetic decoding skills, enabling the reading of an unlimited number of words.

Objective of the Program

The specific objective of the *Phonics Is Fun* program is to provide for mastery of the minimum number of phonetic skills that will assure achievement in word recognition. The sequence in which these skills are developed is based on the frequency with which phonetic elements occur in the English language.

Instruction is accomplished through a multisensory approach. Activities include auditory, visual, and tactile discrimination exercises, as well as sound blending, word pronunciation, reading, spelling, and writing words within the context of sentences.

Characteristics of the Program

The focus of *Phonics Is Fun* is not memorization of phonetic axioms. Instead, the emphasis is for the child to identify elements the phonetic principles address, state rules in personal language, and apply each rule, tip, and definition to appropriate words.

Phonics Is Fun, Book 1, presents the recognition of the letters of the alphabet, single consonants, short and long vowels, *Y* as a vowel, consonant blends, consonant digraphs, and endings *-s, -ed*, and *-ing*.

Phonics Is Fun, Book 2, reviews and extends the skills taught in *Book 1*. It also introduces hard and soft *C* and *G*, *W* as a vowel, vowel digraphs, vowels with *R*, affixes, contractions, synonyms, antonyms, and homonyms.

Phonics Is Fun, Book 3, reviews and broadens the skills taught in *Book 1* and *Book 2* prior to presenting syllabication.

The acquisition of phonetic skills is cumulative in nature, with subsequent levels of instruction building on prior teaching. The following phonetic rules are developed in *Books 1* and *2* of *Phonics Is Fun*, then are expanded upon in *Book 3*: *Short Vowel Rule, Long Vowel Rule 1, Long Vowel Rule 2, Y as a Consonant, Y as Long I, Y as Long E, Vowel W Rule, Soft C Rule*, and *Soft G Rule*. Rules, tips, and definitions are explicitly defined in appropriate lessons in the Teacher's Manual.

Implementing the Program

This Teacher's Edition presents lesson plans that can be used effectively with an individual child, a small group, or an entire class. Each activity is designated with a boldface title to be easily located. You can choose activities based on time considerations, availability of materials, and academic needs. (For instance, you might conduct the activities in some lessons over the span of two class sessions.) Recommended materials are common to most classrooms. Preparation options are suggested when appropriate, and an effort has been made to include the children in these preparations.

The lesson plans contain the following sections: Assessment, Review, Teaching Ideas, Reteaching, and Extension. The first lesson in each book will begin with an Assessment activity. A Review section appears only when the reteaching of an earlier skill will help the child grasp the new concept presented in the Teaching Ideas section. Skills are developed in Teaching Ideas, redeveloped in Reteaching, and enriched in Extension. While the activities in Teaching Ideas are intended for implementation with the entire class, the Reteaching and Extension exercises are directed to the individual child. Reduced facsimiles of Pupil Edition pages appear on the same page as the corresponding lesson to insure that specific practice follows immediately after instruction.

Involving the Family

Family Involvement Letters are referenced in most teaching units and are provided at the back of each Teacher's Edition for duplication. The activities suggested in these letters are designed to acquaint families with the work their child is doing in *Phonics Is Fun*, and to provide further review and reinforcement of the skills. Families choosing to participate in these activities will find each activity presented in a step-by-step format, with materials that involve little preparation and are common to most homes. While participation in these activities is not mandatory, the teacher may choose to use submitted projects as part of the classroom display or materials.

Contents

Lesson 1
The Alphabet *A* through *Z*   (pages 1–2)

Objective   The child will identify the letters *A* through *Z* in sequence and in mixed order.

Assessment

Listening   To practice rhyming skills, ask the children to identify each pair of rhyming words in each of the following sentences.

1. *Do not waste the paste.*
2. *Two boys have the same name.*
3. *A guide will show you where to go.*

Teaching Ideas

Listening   Distribute a set of printed letter cards for the capital letters. Ask the children to place the letter cards one at a time on the chalkboard ledge in alphabetical order. Ask the children to say the alphabet as you point to each letter card. Then distribute the letter cards for the small letters. Ask the children to come to the chalkboard, in turn, to find the partner capital letter for each letter card and to place the small letter card on top of its partner letter card. You may want the children to say the letter name aloud holding up the partner letter for the rest of the children to see.

Distribute the printed letter cards for both the capital and small letters. Display a set of cursive letter cards on the chalkboard ledge. Ask volunteers to place their letters on the corresponding letters in the displayed cursive alphabet. Ask the children to name each cursive letter.

Writing   Write a letter of the alphabet on the chalkboard. Invite a volunteer to write on the chalkboard the letters that precede and follow the one you wrote. Reinforce the accurate responses by inviting the child to write a different letter to begin the activity again.

Speaking   You may have the children work in pairs for this activity. Distribute a letter card to one child. Have the child conceal the identity of the letter card and provide a challenging, yet clear, description of the letter to the other child. You might suggest an example such as, *This capital letter looks like a tent with a stick across the middle* (A). Acknowledge the descriptions as well as the answers.

Reteaching

Tactile   You may want to select capital and small letters from a textured alphabet made of wood, felt, or plastic. Encourage each child to trace one letter with eyes closed, and name it. Have the child confirm the choice with eyes open. Continue with additional letters.

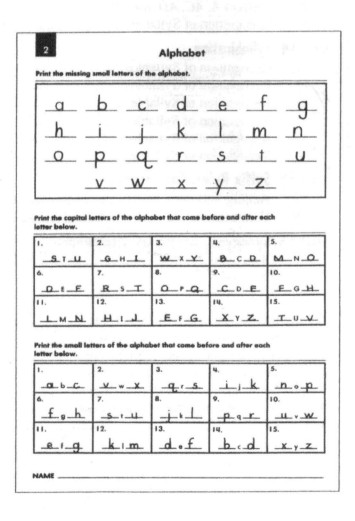

Lesson 2
Consonant Sounds D, S, T, Z, B, F, P, and V   (pages 3–6)

Objective   The child will identify the letters D, S, T, Z, B, F, P, and V and their respective sounds within words.

Review

Speaking   To provide the children with practice in recognizing cursive letters, write the following words in cursive on the chalkboard, then ask volunteers to spell each word aloud.

streets	*kindness*	*express*	*avoid*
inquire	*repeat*	*unreal*	*acquit*
disgrace	*accept*	*distrust*	*admit*

Teaching Ideas

Listening   Say the following words, stressing the beginning sound in each, and ask the children to identify the sound: *deer, diving, dolphin, desk, dish.* You may wish to write two of the words on the chalkboard, underlining the *d* to

reinforce letter/sound associations. Continue the activity by using groups of words such as the following: *sun, soup, seven, salad; table, turkey, team, television; zipper, zoo, zero, zebra.*

Say the following words and ask for volunteers to identify the ending consonant sound heard in each: *hand, dress, heart, breeze, sled, glass, goat, froze.*

You may wish to follow the same procedure to introduce the remaining consonant sounds. Invite the children to identify the initial sound in the following groups of words: *blob, basket, bee, book; food, family, fish, feather; people, paper, pickle, polite; violet, vase, vote, very.*

Complete the activity by pronouncing the following words and asking the children to identify the ending consonant heard in each: *chief, hoop, serve, loaf, stamp, brave, web.*

Pantomime Game   Invite the children to play the Pantomime Game. Put slips of paper containing the following words into a box.

drumming	*diving*	*driving*	*typing*
tying	*boxing*	*batting*	*smiling*
swimming	*flying*	*fishing*	*skateboarding*
painting	*polishing*	*patting*	

Write the letters *D, T, B, S, F,* and *P* on the chalkboard, explaining that the letters represent the consonant sounds that begin each action word the children will act out. Ask for a volunteer to select a piece of paper out of the box and perform the suggested action for the rest of the class. Encourage the child who guesses the action correctly to become the next

performer. When the children have used all the slips of paper, you might challenge them to suggest additional actions. Encourage the performers as well as the guessers.

Extension

Writing   You may wish to write the following words on the chalkboard, or have the child write them on a piece of paper as part of the activity: *dog, zoo, boy, toy, vase, dive, sun, pig, bunny, zip*. Write the letters *D, S, T, Z, B, F, P,* and *V* on the chalkboard, and encourage the child to substitute one consonant for the initial letter in each word to create a new word. You might challenge the child to make more than one change in a word, as in *zip*.

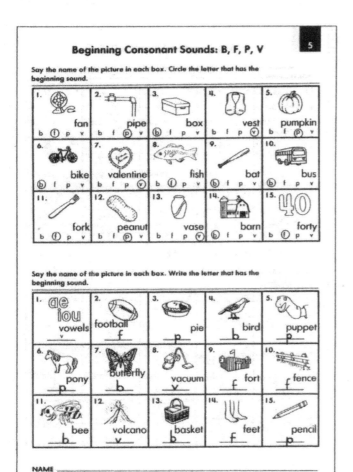

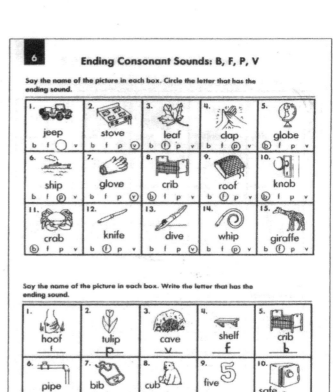

Lesson 3
Consonant Sounds C, G, H, J, K, M, N, and QU (pages 7–9)

Objective   The child will identify the letters C, G, H, J, K, M, N, and Qu and their respective sounds within words.

Review

Speaking   To practice recognition of the cursive alphabet, display a cursive alphabet chart or letter cards. Invite the children to name the individual letters, capital and small, as you point to them.

Teaching Ideas

Listening   Write the following letters on the chalkboard: C, G, H, J, K, M, N, Qu. Invite volunteers to point to and to name the letter that begins each of the following words you say aloud.

hippo	jeans	cabbage	garage
machine	noise	question	key
hope	joy	music	carrot
game	never	quiz	kitten

Remind the children that Q is always followed by u. Repeat the exercise, asking the children to point to and to name the letter of the ending sound of each of the following words you say aloud.

zigzag	chipmunk	broom	nation
quake	swim	dug	flag
park	storm	chain	rake
balloon			

Speaking   Arrange the following picture flashcards on the chalkboard ledge: *glove, heart, moon, nurse, queen, cap, jacks, kite*. Invite the children to say the picture's name and tell the letters that stand for the beginning and ending sounds. Recognize the children for their participation, and discuss the similarities of incorrect and correct answers. Point out, for example, that C and K often have the same sound.

You may also wish to place the following picture flashcards on the chalkboard ledge: *key, mittens, nurse, queen, jacks, coat, goat, hose*. Ask a volunteer to name the picture on the ledge that rhymes with each of the following.

boat and begins with C	*sea* and begins with K
coat and begins with G	*kittens* and begins with M
rose and begins with H	*purse* and begins with N
cracks and begins with J	*lean* and begins with Qu

Name-the-Card Game   Place the alphabet cards C, G, H, J, K, M, N, and Qu on the chalkboard ledge in view of the children. Organize the children into two teams. Ask a question that can be answered with a word beginning with one of the above letters. Encourage the children on a team to

discuss possible answers. Call on the first team to raise their hands. If you wish, keep score without penalizing incorrect answers. You might use the following questions.

(For *M*)   *What shines in the night sky? (moon)*

(For *G* or *J*)   *What do we see in the zoo? (gorillas, goats, jaguars)*

(For *Qu*)   *What is another word for fast? (quick)*

(For *K*)   *What do we use to open a lock? (key)*

(For *C*)   *What does Bugs Bunny like to eat? (carrots)*

(For *H*)   *If we call a girl "her," what do we call a boy? (him)*

(For *N*)   *What is twelve o'clock during the day called? (noon)*

You might further challenge the children by having one team create the questions for the other team.

Listening/Speaking   Say the following sentences and invite the children to name the words that begin with the sound indicated.

C: Cathy fed cabbage and carrots to the hamster.

G: The gorilla dropped the grapes to the ground.

H: A heavy flowerpot hung next to the hammock.

J: Jason joined the children jumping rope.

K: We keep an extra key on the hook in the kitchen.

M: Melissa gave us money to buy magazines at the mall.

N: The narrow, unpaved street was noisy every night.

Qu: Amy quarreled with Rachel about the questions on the quiz.

Writing   Write the letters *g, k, m*, and *n* and the following incomplete words on the chalkboard: *boo __ , fro __ , ope __ , loo __ , hu __ , cloc __ , ba __ , ru __ , bea __* . Ask for volunteers to write one of the consonants from the lesson to complete a word, and then say the word aloud. When all the words have been completed, challenge the children to suggest different consonants (not included in this lesson) to end each word.

Extension

Writing   Ask the child to write the letters *C, G, H, J, K, M, N*, and *Qu* across the top of a sheet of paper. Challenge the child to list three objects or names that end with each of the letters. If the child seems to be having difficulty, suggest that the names of people or objects in the classroom might provide examples.

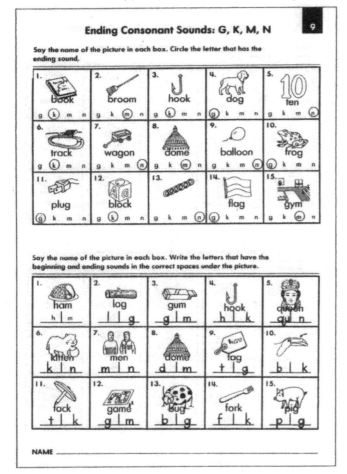

Lesson 4
Consonant Sounds *L, R, W, Y,* and *X* (pages 10–12)

Objective   The child will identify the sounds of *L, R, W, Y,* and *X* appearing in isolation and within words.

Review

Memory Game   To exercise the children's auditory discrimination, play the Memory Game. Write the following letters on the chalkboard: *B, C, D, F, G, H, J, K, M, N, P, Q, S, T, V, Z.* Begin the game with a statement such as *I went to Washington and in my trunk I took a ....* Then name an item that begins with the sound of *B.* Explain that each child will have an opportunity, in turn, to add an item to this statement beginning with each subsequent letter listed on the chalkboard. Point out, however, that each child must first repeat, in order, all items previously named before adding a new item to the list. Players who omit an item from the list, or who do not name an item with the designated letter, are eliminated from play. Let play continue—repeating the list of beginning sounds if necessary—until all of the children have had a turn.

Teaching Ideas

Listening   Write the letters *L, R, W, Y,* and *X* in cursive on the chalkboard. Direct students to listen carefully for the beginning sound as you read a list of words beginning with one of the targeted letters. Consider using the following lists of words.

- *L: light, list, learn, listen, library*
- *R: rabbit, rocket, round, ring, record*
- *W: well, wise, web, winter, wax*
- *Y: yo-yo, yawn, yes, yell, yarn*
- *X: (You might ask the children to suggest a word beginning with X, such as x-ray, because there are so few of these words.)*

Have each child raise a hand when the targeted sound is recognized. Invite a volunteer to name the sound. You might then challenge the child to name another word beginning with the same sound. Continue with another word list until you have offered words beginning with *L, R, W,* and *Y.* To check for auditory perception of these consonants as the final sounds, use the same procedure with the following lists.

- *L: hill, bill, wall, sell, bell*
- *R: car, door, spare, deer, rooster*
- *X: wax, ox, Tex, ax*

You might conclude this activity by reviewing the targeted sounds in mixed order, inviting volunteers to identify the

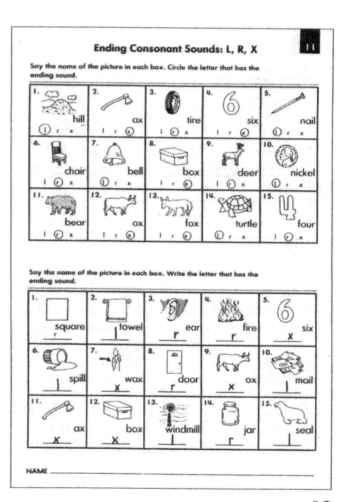

beginning consonant in each of the following words: *lamp, rice, wigwam, yard, lettuce, red, wash, yellow.*

Writing   Write these sentences on the chalkboard, omitting the answers in parentheses.

1. *Tom forgot to mail the __ etter. (l)*
2. *We have to wash and wa __ the car. (x)*
3. *My favorite colors are blue, __ ed, and green. (r)*
4. *We like to play in the __ ard. (y)*
5. *The spider spins a __ eb. (w)*

For each, ask a child to read the sentence to identify the missing letter. To involve more children, you might let the child call on a classmate who will go to the board, fill in the letter, and reread the sentence.

Pantomime Game   Play the Pantomime Game, described in Lesson 2 of this unit, using words that begin with the consonant sounds L, R, W, and Y. Prepare cards with the following words: *L: looking, leaning; R: reading, running; W: walking, washing; Y: yawning, yelling.* Encourage the other children to guess the action being pantomimed. You might invite the child who guesses the action to be the next actor.

Listening   Since the consonant sound of X does not lend itself as readily to the previous activities, you may want to do the following exercise. Read each of the following sentences aloud.

1. *You must excuse yourself the next time.*
2. *Tex hopes to save exactly sixty cents.*
3. *The children became excited when they saw the taxi.*
4. *Sixteen and sixty are numbers.*
5. *The ox roared extremely loud when it saw the ax.*

For each sentence, appoint one child to be the "Listener" and a second child to be the "Checker." After you have read the sentence aloud, ask the listener to name all the words in the sentence that have the X sound. (You might repeat each sentence several times to assist the listeners.) Then ask the Checker to confirm whether the listener correctly identified all the words with the sound.

Consider writing the sentences on tagboard strips and appointing a student reader for each sentence.

Extension

Prize-List Game   Tell the child to imagine winning a prize on a game show. As a winner, the child can choose two items that begin with each of the following letters: L, R, W, and Y. Have the child write out a list of the eight items he or she would take. If more than one child participates, you might have the children share and compare their lists.

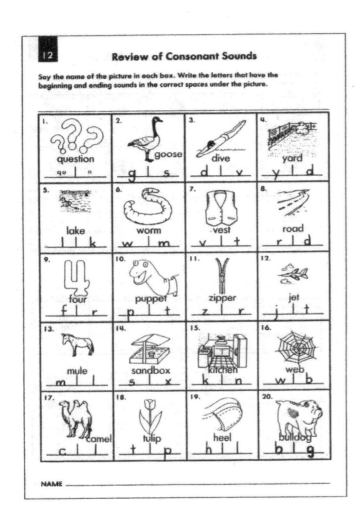

Lesson 5
Short Vowel A (pages 13–15)

Objective   The child will identify the short sound of *A* and read short *A* words appearing in isolation and within sentences.

Short Vowel Rule: If a word or a syllable has only one vowel, and it comes at the beginning or between two consonants, the vowel is usually short.

Review

Surprise-Box Game   To review recognition of the consonants, divide the children into two teams to play this game. Place cards showing the consonant letters of the alphabet in a bag or box. Call on a player from each team to watch as you draw a letter out at random. Let the child who is first to name the letter and give a word that begins with that consonant earn a team point. You might offer bonus points to a child who can think of a word that ends with the consonant. Continue until all the letters have been drawn.

Teaching Ideas

Speaking   Consider using a deductive approach to develop the sound of short vowel *A*. Write the following words in two rows on the chalkboard: *ant/apple/axle/ask, hand/catch/jack/lamp*. Have the children repeat each word after you as you read it. Then challenge the children to identify the one sound that all eight words share. Encourage children to pronounce the sound as well as to name it Short Vowel *A*.

Ask if the placement of the letter *A* in the first set of words is different from its place in the second set. (The first set has *A* at the beginnings of the words; the second set has *A* between two consonants.) Encourage the children to express the Short Vowel Rule in their own words.

Take-It-Out Game   To develop auditory discrimination skills, read aloud each of the following lists of words: *pan/pat/pick/pack, Sam/Dan/Jake/Jack, Dad/Dan/damp/dig, fine/fat/flat/flap, bag/big/bat/batch*. For each list, ask a child to identify the one word in the list that should be taken out because it does not have the short *A* sound.

Consider inviting several children to work independently to create additional lists. Point out that the four words in each set should begin with the same consonant sound and that three of the four words should use the short *A* sound. To reward their efforts, give children who made lists an opportunity to read their lists aloud and invite classmates to identify the inappropriate word in each list.

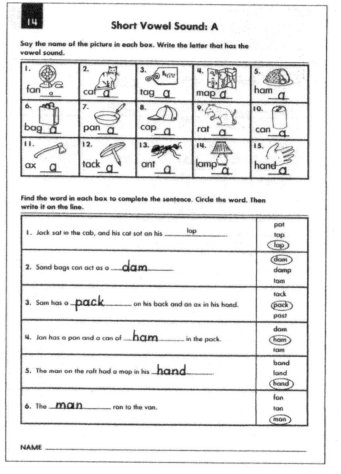

Writing   Write the following words and incomplete sentences on the chalkboard.

fan   gas   bag   man   sad   bat   cat

1. *Please fill the car with* _____ .
2. *When my friend moved away, I felt* _____ .
3. *His father is a very nice* _____ .
4. *To cool the room, we turn on the* _____ .
5. *There are some cookies in the* _____ .
6. *Sam has two pets, a dog and a* _____ .
7. *To play baseball, you need a ball and a* _____ .

Invite volunteers to each read an incomplete sentence and to select the word from the list that best completes it. Have the child write the correct word on the line and reread the sentence.

Extension

Lotto Game   For extended practice in recognizing the short *A* sound, have a child make a lotto board and then play the game. To make the board, offer the child a word bank consisting of the following word cards.

tag	*tack*	*tap*	*can*	*cap*	*cab*
man	*ramp*	*map*	*bag*	*sack*	*wax*
tax	*ax*	*hat*	*bat*	*fact*	*lamp*
lamb	*hand*	*band*	*rat*	*fan*	*fat*

Help the child to divide an unlined sheet of paper into nine squares by folding it in thirds lengthwise, fold it in thirds along the width, and draw lines along the folds. Then have the child write a different word from the list in each square. Point out that words should be picked randomly. When the child has completed the board, put the full set of word cards into the sack and give the child a pile of paper markers or small chips. Let the child draw a card randomly from the bag and read it aloud. Words appearing on the child's board should be covered with a marker. Have the game end when all the words on the board are covered. Consider having several children make lotto boards and play together.

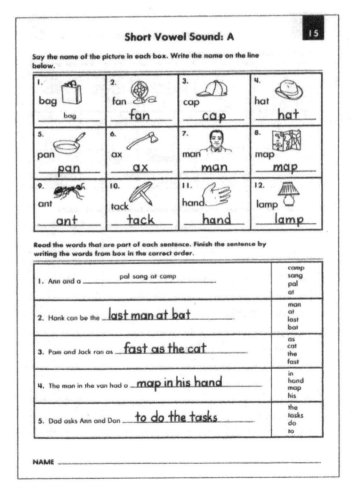

Lesson 6
Short Vowel I (pages 16–18)

Objective   The child will identify the short sound of *I* and will read short *I* words appearing in isolation and within sentences.

Review

Longest-List Game   You might use the following co-operative learning game to review the children's awareness of the short *A* sound. Group the children into teams of three or four. Give the groups five minutes to draw up a list of items that have the short *A* sound and can be found in a house. You might suggest *pan* and *can* as starting words for each list. At the end of the appointed time, have the children determine which team has thought of the most words. Award a point for each word. You might want to make a rule that the teams lose a point if they include a word that does not use the short *A* sound.

Teaching Ideas

Listening   To develop the short sound of *I* using an approach similar to that described in Lesson 5, write the following words on the chalkboard: *itch/is/if, pick/grin/dish.* Ask which sound can be found in all six words. Then ask where the vowel is placed in each of the two sets of words. Use the

children's responses to encourage them to express the Short Vowel Rule in their own words.

Take-It-Out Game   To develop auditory discrimination of the short *I* sound, play the Take-It-Out Game described in Lesson 5 in this unit. Consider using the following word sets.

> *mill/miss/mitt/mat*   *Kim/Bill/Sam/Tim*
> *lip/lap/lift/lick*   *sack/sick/still/sit*
> *pig/pack/pick/pit*

You might also reinforce awareness of the short *A* sound by challenging the children to identify the vowel sound in the word that is to be taken out.

You-Name-It Game   Play the following drawing game to give children practice in recognizing words with short *A* and short *I* sounds. Prepare the following word cards: *fan, lip, rabbit, windmill, glass, pig, stamp, gift, hill.* Invite a volunteer to come forward, choose a card, and draw picture clues for the word. Explain that the person drawing the picture cannot give any verbal clues but must rely on drawing to communicate. You may want to remind the guessers that the answer will always be a word that uses the short *A* or the short *I* sound. Once the word is guessed, have the artist label the picture. You may want to let the child who correctly identifies the word choose the next card.

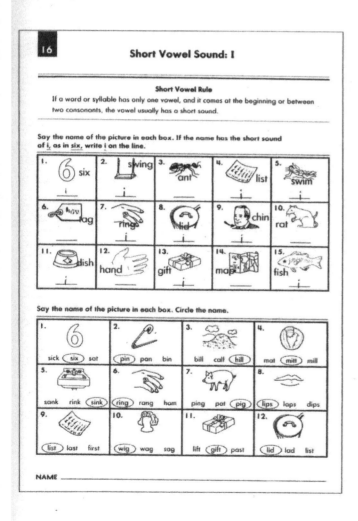

Reteaching

Reading   Write the following six sentences on the chalkboard.

1. *Six pigs ran into an anthill.*
2. *We hid his gift in the kitchen.*
3. *Jill had her ring on her finger.*
4. *Here is my list of gifts.*
5. *Pin that red tag to the wig.*
6. *Bill hid the kit under the bed.*

For each sentence, have the child read the sentence aloud, circle all the short *I* words, and draw a box around the short *A* words.

Extension

Wish-List Art   Invite the child to create a wish list by finding and cutting out pictures of three to six things the child would like to own. Direct the child to pick only items with names that have the short vowel *I* or *A* sounds. Offer the child old magazines, catalogs, or advertising inserts from the newspaper as a source for material. Have the child arrange and label the pictures on a sheet of paper. Give special recognition to the child who does an especially creative job of presenting the wish list.

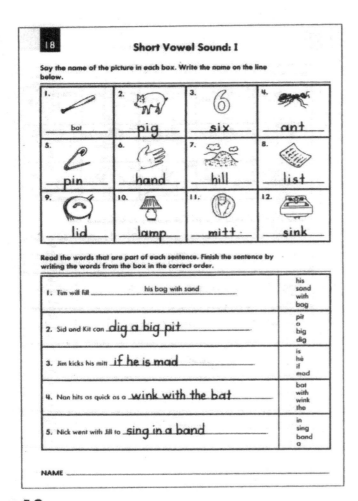

Lesson 7
Short Vowel *U*   (pages 19–21)

Objective   The child will identify the short sound of *U* and will read short *U* words appearing in isolation and within sentences.

Review

Speaking   To practice recognition of short *I* and short *A*, write the following words as the heads of columns on the chalkboard: *tan, hit, cat, tip.* Invite volunteers to each think of a new short *A* or short *I* word that can be formed by changing the beginning consonant of one of the key words. (For example, *tan* can be changed to *can.*) Reinforce a correct response by letting the child write the new word in the appropriate column on the chalkboard. Acknowledge the child who recognizes that changing the initial sounds results in a list of rhyming words.

Teaching Ideas

Listening   Continue the procedure in the Review by writing the words *up* and *us* on the chalkboard. Challenge the children to think of at least two rhyming words for each (*cup/sup/pup/hiccup, bus/fuss/plus/discuss*). Invite the children to write correct responses on the chalkboard. When the words have been recorded, ask a volunteer to identify the common vowel sounds in each of the words. Reinforce the correct answer by having the child circle the *U* in each of the words on the chalkboard. Continue by asking the difference between the placement of the *U* in the two key words and where it appears in the rhyming words. (It is at the beginning of the key words and between two consonants in the other words.) Ask a volunteer to explain the short vowel sound in both sets of words. Encourage the children to apply the Short Vowel Rule in their own words.

Take-It-Out Game   To develop auditory discrimination of the short *U* sound, play the Take-It-Out Game described in Lesson 5 in this unit. Consider using the following word sets: *run/sun/bun/tan, bus/bun/bit/but, tug/tag/jug/rug, bin/bun/run/fun.* Assist children in identifying the short vowel sound of the word that is to be taken out.

Pass-It-On Story Game   You may wish to prepare word cards for the following short *U* words: *bump, hunt, truck, just, sun, upon, club, trunk, struck.* Place the cards in a bag. Explain that you are going to begin to tell a story and that you will "Pass It On" to a child, who will continue the story by describing what happens next. Point out that each subsequent storyteller must choose one of the words from the bag, show it to the class, and then continue the story using that word on the card. After one or two sentences, invite another volunteer to continue following the same procedure, choosing a new word card to include in the story. You might repeat the activity with another set of short *U* words.

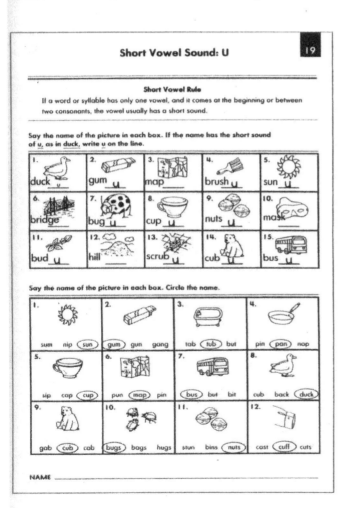

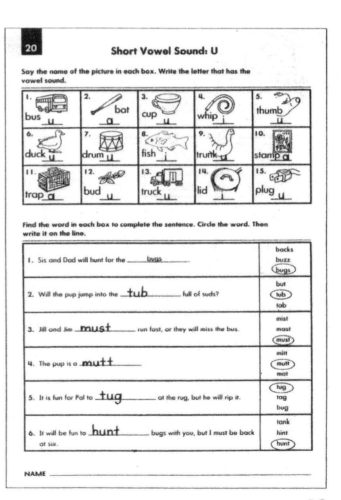

Writing   Write the following incomplete sentences on the chalkboard.

1. *Bud likes to sit in the _____ .   (sun)*
2. *The dog _____ a hole.   (dug)*
3. *A boat that pulls another boat is called a _____ .   (tug)*
4. *Gus thinks it is fun to ride on the school _____ .   (bus)*
5. *The pup likes to curl up on the _____ that covers the floor.   (rug)*

Challenge the children to work independently, copying the sentences on paper and thinking of a short *U* word that would complete each sentence. Invite volunteers to each read a completed sentence aloud. If children have difficulty with a sentence, consider offering a clue by giving them the initial consonant sound of the word. Help children apply the Short Vowel Rule to explain the short *U* sound in each of the missing words. (Save the sentences for use in the Reteaching activity that follows.)

Reteaching

Writing   Ask the child to circle all the words in the previous writing activity that have the short *U* sound.

Short Vowel Sound: U   21

Say the name of the picture in each box. Write the name on the line below.

1. cub	2. bus	3. tub	4. cup
5. gum	6. sun	7. lamp	8. duck
9. pig	10. cuff	11. nuts	12. bugs

Read the words that are part of each sentence. Finish the sentence by writing the words from the box in the correct order.

1. Is Kim _____ill with the mumps_____ ?	with / mumps / ill / the
2. The big tank _is full of rust_____	rust / is / of / full
3. Dan must jump up to _pick up the cup_____	up / the / cup / pick
4. A pack of gum was at the _back of the bus_	bus / the / back / of
5. The bus dug a _rut in the mud_____	the / in / rut / mud

NAME _____

20

Lesson 8
Short Vowel O (pages 22–24)

Objective   The child will read short *O* words appearing in isolation and within sentences.

Review

Writing   To review short *A*, *I*, and *U*, write the following incomplete words on the chalkboard.

```
s__t    p__g    h__m    b__s
c__n    t__p    w__n    m__n
p__n    g__m    t__x    b__g
```

For each, have a volunteer complete the word with an *A*, *I*, or *U*, and use the word in a sentence. Encourage children to think of more than one way to complete the word using the targeted letters (*sit/sat, ham/him/hum, tap/tip, pan/pin/pun, bag/big/bug*).

Teaching Ideas

Listening   To introduce the short *O* sound, turn the classroom lights off and on. Ask a volunteer to describe your action. When a child answers correctly, write the words *off* and *on* on the chalkboard and identify the vowel sound as the short *O* sound. Continue by writing these additional words on the chalkboard: *block, spot, stop*. Ask the children to identify the vowel in these words. When a child answers correctly, ask the child to describe the location of the the short *O* in each of the words. Challenge the children to apply the Short Vowel Rule in their own words.

Speaking/Writing   You may wish to prepare the following word cards for short *O* words: *dock, frog, clock, spot, Bobby, doll*. For each, ask a volunteer to read the word and use it in a sentence. Then let the child pick a classmate who will write the sentence on the chalkboard and underline the words with the sound of short *O*. Encourage children to think of sentences that include more than one short *O* word.

Catch-a-Card Game   Play the Catch-a-Card Game with the following word cards: *fox, dog, jot, lost, lock, not, ox, socks, spot, stop*. Direct nine children to place their chairs in a row at the front of the room. Call on a tenth child to stand behind the child sitting in the first chair. Flash a word card to both children. The first child to respond correctly keeps the word card. That child then stands behind the child sitting in the next chair, while the child who was not the correct respondent in the first match is seated in the first chair. Let the game continue with the remaining words. When the cards have all been claimed, have the children each read their word cards one at a time. You may want to declare the child with the most cards the champion.

Take-It-Out Game   To develop auditory discrimination of the short *O* sound, play the Take-It-Out Game, as described in Lesson 5 in this unit. Consider using the following word sets.

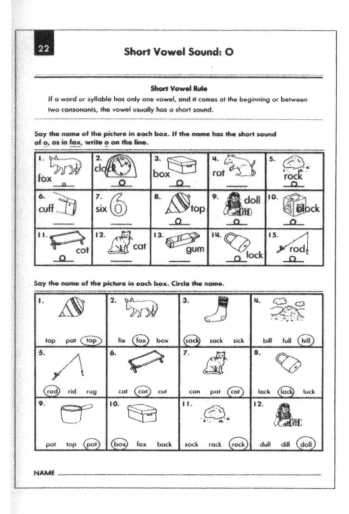

mop/box/top/tap   *rock/sock/sack/lock*
lost/last/lock/log   *tip/top/stop/crop*

Challenge the children to identify the short vowel sound in the word that is to be taken out.

Listening   Write the following sentences on the chalkboard.

1. *We saw a frog in the pond.*
2. *Please put the top on the box.*
3. *Bob does not like his job.*
4. *He lost his left sock.*
5. *The dog slept on the cot.*

Appoint a listener and a checker for each sentence. Direct the two to listen carefully as you read the sentence twice. After the second reading, have the listener write all the words in the sentence that have the short *O* sound on the chalkboard. Point out that the checker is to confirm that all appropriate words have been identified. (Save the sentences for use in the Extension activity that follows.)

Extension

Writing   Offer the child a list of the following short *O* words: *off, on, top, sock, dog, fox, box, on, rock, pond, frog, Bob, Todd, Don, Donna.* Challenge the child to see how many of these words—or other short *O* words—can be included in the same sentence. You might use the sentences in the listening exercise above as a model. Encourage the child to make the sentence interesting or amusing. You may want to have the child illustrate an especially creative sentence.

24

Short Vowel Sound: O

Say the name of the picture in each box. Write the name on the line below.

1. box	2. rod	3. sun	4. gum
5. mop	6. lamp	7. top	8. pot
9. hill	10. fox	11. doll	12. rock

Read the words that are part of each sentence. Finish the sentence by writing the words from the box in the correct order.

1. Mom has _____ a job for Bob _____.	for / a / job / Bob
2. Dot cannot lift the hot pot _____.	the / lift / hot / pot
3. Jill got rid of the box of junk _____.	junk / of / the / box
4. The dog cannot jump on the cot _____.	jump / the / cot / on
5. It is not odd to see a lot of rocks on the hill _____.	rocks / hill / the / on

NAME _____

22

Lesson 9
Short Vowel *E* (pages 25–27)

Objective The child will identify the short sound of *E* and read short *E* words appearing in isolation and within sentences.

Review

Twenty-Questions Game To review short *A*, *I*, *U*, and *O*, prepare the following word cards for a variation of the classic guessing game, Twenty Questions: *hand, bib, tub, mop, pan, pig, nut*. Invite a volunteer to choose one of the word cards, for example, *hand*. Have the child begin the game by saying, *I am thinking of a word that has the short vowel* A. Explain that the other children are to ask questions to help them guess the word. Point out that questions may refer only to the use or appearance of the item or to the other sounds found in the word, and that all questions must call for *yes* and *no* answers. (For example, *Where can you find it?* is an unacceptable question, but *Can you find it in a store?* is acceptable.) If the answer is not guessed within twenty questions, have the child choose a different card, repeating the same procedure. Otherwise, let the child who correctly guessed the answer be "It" for the next round. You might consider restricting questions to sound clues such as: *Does the word begin with the consonant sound of C?*

Teaching Ideas

Listening Ask the children to tell what a spider spins. When a child responds correctly, write *web* on the chalkboard and circle the *E*. Identify the sound as the short *E* sound. You might display the following word cards: *bed, bell, belt, desk, tent, jet, leg, pet, jet*. Have volunteers each read a word, identifying the vowel sound. Challenge children to explain why the vowel sound is short by applying the Short Vowel Rule.

Speaking/Writing Write the following words on the chalkboard: *best, felt, left, rest, send, tent*. For each, have a child read the word and then use it in a short sentence. Ask a volunteer to write the sentence on the chalkboard, underlining the short *E* words. Encourage children to both use and recognize the use of other short *E* words in the sentences.

Catch-a-Card Game Play the Catch-a-Card Game, described in Lesson 8 in this unit, using the following word cards: *bell, belt, den, pet, fell, get, help, hem, let, kept*. Make the game more challenging by asking the winners to use each word they have won in a sentence.

Following Directions To give the children practice in following oral directions as they work on vowel and consonant sounds, write the following words in three columns on the chalkboard.

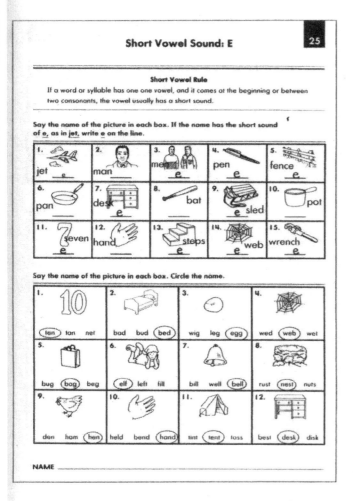

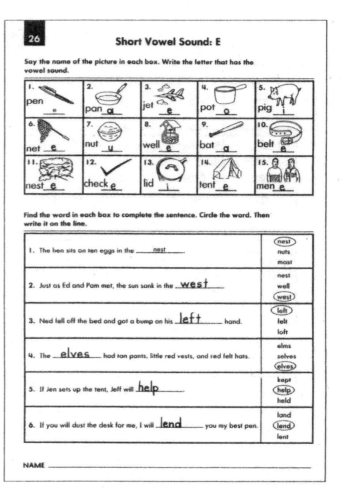

23

bell	*bet*	*beg*
hem	*fell*	*yet*
pen	*went*	*led*
pet	*hen*	*leg*

Direct the children to work independently, writing the words in the first column and then changing the vowel in each word to make a new word. You might have a volunteer model the directions for the first word, for example, *bell* can be changed to *ball, bill,* or *bull.* Allow ample time for the activity to be completed. Then encourage volunteers to read the new words they have formed. Have some children write the new words on the chalkboard. Challenge the children to think of more than one new word.

Continue by giving a different set of directions for the words in the second column. Tell the children that for these words, they are to change each beginning consonant to form new words. (For example, *bet* could become *pet, wet, let,* or *set.*) Again, have the children work independently, sharing their results as above. Encourage the children to think of more than one new word or to recognize that each set of new words in this column rhyme. Finally, follow the same procedure for the words in the third column, but direct the children to change the ending consonant in each to form a new word, for example, *beg* could become *bet* or *bed.* (You may wish to save the words on the chalkboard for the Extension activity.)

Extension

Writing   Invite a child to use the words from the previous activity as a word bank to write a sentence that includes as many short vowel *E* words as possible. Give extra recognition to the child for thinking of a rhyming sentence or set of sentences by reading these to the class.

Short Vowel Sound: E   27

Say the name of the picture in each box. Write the name on the line below.

1.	2.	3.	4.
ten	net	web	bed
5.	6.	7.	8.
man	tent	jet	hen
9.	10.	11.	12.
well	men	elf	desk

Read the words that are part of each sentence. Finish the sentence by writing the words from the box in the correct order.

1. The big elk _____ sped by the men _____	by men the sped
2. Ted's well-fed pet is _a big red hen_	red big o hen
3. Jeff has the mumps, but he _will get well fast_	fast get well will
4. Tell Bess to mend the big rip _in Meg's red tent_	Meg's in tent red
5. Meg went on a trip _in a big jet_	o jet big in

NAME _____

Lesson 10
Short Vowel Compound Words and Two-syllable Words (page 28)

Objective The child will identify the syllables in two-syllable words containing short-vowel sounds.

Review

How-Many-Words? Game To practice recognition of the short vowels *A, I, O,* and *E,* write the word *apologetic* on the chalkboard. Allow five minutes for each child to work independently, finding and writing down short-vowel words that can be formed from the letters of this word. At the end of the designated time, determine which child has identified the most words. Invite that child to read the list as you record the words on the chalkboard. Disqualify any words that do not have a short vowel sound, such as *eat.* After the winner's list has been recorded, invite children to name any additional words that might be thought of and then added to the list, including the following.

at	act	cap	cot	get	got
it	leg	let	lit	lip	log
lot	peg	pet	pelt	pig	pit
pot	tag	tap	tip	top	cat

Teaching Ideas

Listening Write the following words on the chalkboard: *sunset, dustpan, hilltop, cannot, windmill.* Invite volunteers to identify the two small words that are combined to create each longer word. For each correct response, have the child circle the two smaller words, identifying the vowel sounds in each. Explain that words that are composed of two or more short words are called compound words. Invite the children to use the compound words in original sentences.

Continue to develop the concept of short vowel syllables by writing the following words on the chalkboard: *basket, tennis, hidden, mitten, rabbit, muffin.* Have the children focus on the word *basket.* Explain that even though this word is not composed of two smaller words, it does have two syllables. As you say the word, direct the children to listen for each syllable. Have a volunteer draw a line to show the syllable break. Explain that in many two-syllable words, the syllable break comes between two consonants located in the middle of the word. Invite volunteers to read and mark the breaks between the remaining five two-syllable words on the chalkboard.

Where's-the-Rest-of-My-Word? Game Display the following word cards on the chalkboard ledge: *fish, hill, dog, self, tub, bag.* Then distribute the following word cards to the children: *hand, bath, him, cat, up, bull.* Direct these children to each find a card on the chalkboard ledge that can be combined with the words on their cards to create a compound word. When all the cards have been chosen, let these children each show their two cards to the class and read the resulting compound word. Encourage children to use the compound word in a sentence.

Extension

Writing Provide the following word cards: *hand, sand, him, her, it, can, dust, pig, up, sun, cuffs, box, self, not, pan, pen, hill, set, web, bag, cob.* Invite the child to create compound words by combining two of the word cards. Have the child display the two cards together in the correct order on a desktop. You might suggest that the child write a list of each compound that is formed. Help the child recognize that some small words may be part of more than one compound, as in the following examples: *handbag/handcuffs, himself/herself/it-self.*

Family Involvement Activity Duplicate the Family Letter on page 91 of this Teacher's Edition. Send it home with the children.

---

28 **Short Vowel Compound Words**

A compound word is made up of two or more one-syllable words. Circle each one-syllable word in the compound words below.

1.	2.	3.	4.	5.	6.
sandbox	bedbug	muskrat	dustpan	uphill	airplane
7.	8.	9.	10.	11.	12.
cobweb	pickax	hatpin	itself	handbag	football
13.	14.	15.	16.	17.	18.
himself	cannot	hilltop	sunset	padlock	bellhop
19.	20.	21.	22.	23.	24.
cockpit	pigpen	upset	bulldog	handcuffs	windmill

Find the compound word in each box to complete the sentence. Circle the word. Then write the word on the line.

1. Jan and Ken ran ____uphill____ to the sandbox.	replace / (uphill) / hilltop	
2. The bulldog was __upset__ by the muskrat.	uphill / sunset / (upset)	
3. Tess will look into the __cockpit__ of the jet.	(cockpit) / cobweb / cannot	
4. Edwin cannot unlock the __padlock__ .	pigpen / pickax / (padlock)	
5. The handbag held a set of __handcuffs__ .	windmills / himself / (handcuffs)	
6. We dusted the __cobwebs__ from the ceiling.	cockpit / (cobwebs) / dustpans	

NAME _____

Lesson 11
Long Vowels *A* and *I*   (pages 29–31)

Objective   The child will apply Long Vowel Rule 1 to long *A* and long *I* words and will read these words in isolation and within sentences.

Long Vowel Rule 1: If one syllable has two vowels, the first vowel is usually long and the second is usually silent.

Review

Speaking   To recall short *A*, short *I*, and the Short Vowel Rule, write the following words on the chalkboard: *at, pan, cap, ran, pin, kit, hid*. For each word, invite a volunteer to read the word and explain why the vowel is short.

Teaching Ideas

Listening   Use the words from the Review activity above to introduce long *A*, long *I*, and the Long Vowel Rule 1. Circle the words *at* and *pan*, directing the children to watch as you change these two words by adding a letter to each. Write the words *ate* and *pain* below the words you circled and pro-nounce them. Ask a child to tell the difference in vowel sounds between *at* and *ate* and between *pan* and *pain*. Explain that the sound of the vowel in each of these new words is the long *A* sound. Continue by asking how many vowels are in the two short *A* words and how many vowels are in the two long *A* words. Ask if the second vowel can be heard in the long *A* words. In this way, encourage the children to express Long Vowel Rule 1 in their own words. For additional practice in forming and recognizing words with long *A* or long *I*, invite volunteers to add an *E* to each of the following words from the Review activity: *cap, pin, kit, hid*. As each word is changed, ask the child to read the new word, and to apply Long Vowel Rule 1 to explain why the vowel sound has changed.

To draw special attention to words in which the final *Y* acts as a vowel, you might write the following words on the chalkboard: *hay, day, way, may*. Have a volunteer read the words and identify the vowel sound in each. Explain that Long Vowel Rule 1 applies to these words because *Y* serves as a silent vowel when it is added to *A* at the end of a one-syllable word.

You may also want to mention that a few words, such as *have* and *give*, are exceptions to Long Vowel Rule 1.

Reading   Write the following sentences on the chalk-board.

Long Vowels: A, I   29

The word cape has the long sound of the vowel a. Say the name of the picture in each box. If the name has the long sound of a, circle the picture.

1. cape 2. cake 3. apple 4. game 5. glass
6. whale 7. table 8. cage 9. camel 10. gate
11. dragon 12. vase 13. shade 14. rake 15. chain
16. stamp 17. stage 18. snake 19. rain 20. car
21. train 22. track 23. grapes 24. mail 25. skate

The word pie has the long sound of the vowel i. Say the name of the picture in each box. If the name has the long sound of i, circle the picture.

1. pie 2. pipe 3. five 4. mitt 5. hive
6. dime 7. ride 8. chin 9. mice 10. iron
11. list 12. tie 13. fire 14. knife 15. spider
16. nine 17. bike 18. windmill 19. lion 20. whirl
21. slide 22. pride 23. vine 24. eight 25. blindfold

NAME

Long Vowel Sounds: A, I   30

Long Vowel Rule I
If a syllable or a one-syllable word has two vowels, the first vowel usually has a long sound and the second vowel is silent.

The short vowel words in the first column of each box have been changed to long vowel words in the second column. Draw a line to join these words.

1. am — aim / pal — paint / can — pail / pant — cane
2. bit — died / did — wine / win — dime / dim — bite
3. cam — come / at — made / mad — ate / van — vane
4. rip — hide / quit — ripe / hid — pine / pin — quite
5. past — rain / man — main / fat — paste / ran — fate
6. kit — time / rid — kite / fin — fine / Tim — ride

Find the word in each box to complete the sentence. Circle the word. Write the word on the line.

1. Her name is Mame, and my name is the ___same___   nine / (same) / name

2. If you bake a cake, may I have a **taste**?   past / haste / (taste)

3. Kit will ___aim___ the ball at the pine tree.   am / dime / (aim)

4. Dave just ate, so he must ___wait___ to dive into the lake.   wide / (wait) / wick

5. The limeade was made with five limes, and it tastes just ___fine___   (fine) / take / fin

6. The last time we went to camp, you lost a pail in the ___lake___   bake / lad / (lake)

NAME

1. *Kate is never late for a date.*
2. *May had a nice time with her kite.*
3. *Jake can ride a mile on his bike.*
4. *Dad will bake Mike a cake.*
5. *Go to the lake and rake the sand.*
6. *Dave has five red ties.*

For each, have a child read the sentence, circle the long *A* words, and underline the long *I* words. Consider appointing a second child as Checker for each sentence to verify that all long *A* and long *I* words have been identified.

Word-Changing Game Prepare the following word cards: *pan, quit, mad, pin, pal, fin, bit, man.* Divide children into two teams. Ask one child from each team to come to the chalkboard. As you flash one of the word cards, challenge each child to add a vowel to make a long vowel word and write it on the chalkboard. Award a point to the team of the first child who responds correctly. Continue calling up pairs of children until all the words have been used. Offer bonus points to a child who is able to form more than one word, for example, *main* and *mane* from *man.*

Reteaching

Reading/Writing To provide additional practice reading sentences with long *A* and *I* words, prepare the following sets of word cards: *likes/bike/to/ride/his, taste/of/the/cake/ had/a, lake/same/went/to/the, nine/has/ties/white.* Then offer

the child one set of the cards along with the following name cards: *Dave, Mike, Jay, Kay, Kate, Fay.* Direct the child to choose one of the name cards, arranging that card with the other five cards to form a sentence that begins with the name. (For example, *Jay likes to ride his bike.*) Have the child read the completed sentences to you, or have the child write the sentences out and circle the long *A* and long *I* words.

Long Vowel Sounds: A, I 31

Say the name of the picture in each box. Then write the missing long vowel.

1. c _a_ ne	2. c _a_ pe	3. b _i_ ke	4. g _a_ te
5. k _i_ te	6. p _a_ il	7. r _i_ de	8. p _i_ e
9. l _a_ ke	10. t _i_ re	11. d _i_ ve	12. r _a_ in

Read the words that are part of each sentence. Finish the sentence by writing the words from the box in the correct order.

1. Elaine's dog likes to ___race to the gate___	to race gate the
2. Jane gave Jack a ___ride on the bike___.	bike on the ride
3. The lions are tame ___and will not bite___	not and will bite
4. Will it take a long time to ___ride to the lake___ ?	to the lake ride
5. Tom, wake up Dave, and tell him ___to make his bed___	his make bed to

NAME _____

27

Lesson 12
Long Vowels *U* and *O*   (pages 32–34)

Objective   The child will apply Long Vowel Rule 1 to long *U* and long *O* words and will read the words in isolation and within sentences.

Review

Catch-Me-If-You-Can Game   Have the children form words containing a designated short vowel as they play the Catch-Me-If-You-Can Game. Divide the class into two teams. Flash a letter card containing one of the vowels to the first player from each team and ask for a word that contains the short sound of that vowel. Award a point to the first child to answer correctly. Have both the children stand at the end of the correct respondent's team line. Continue the game as described until one team line is eliminated or until each child has had at least one turn. For further reinforcement, you might have the child who gives the correct response write the word on the chalkboard.

Teaching Ideas

Listening   To introduce the long vowel sounds of *U* and *O*, ask the children to mention a few of the short *U* and short *O* words that were created in the previous activity. Ask a volunteer to tell why the vowel is short in these words. Then

write *cute* and *use* on the chalkboard. Pronounce the words, repeating the vowel sound. Ask if the vowel sound is the same as the one they heard in the short vowel words. Help the children to recognize that the sounds are different and that the vowel sound in *cute* and *use* is the long vowel sound of *U*. To clarify the application of Long Vowel Rule 1, ask how many vowels are in the long vowel words. Then ask whether the second vowel sound is heard. Use the same procedure with *road* and *code* to introduce the long *O* sound.

Stand-Up-Long, Sit-Down-Short Game   To exercise auditory discrimination skills, place two chairs back-to-back in front of the room so that the children sitting on them cannot see each other. Invite a child to sit in each chair. Then pronounce words such as the following: *tube, rod, cut, coat, toad, tub, rose, cute, due, bone, dome, Sue, rust, rule, snow, mule.* For each word, direct these children to stand if the vowel sound is long and to sit if the vowel sound is short. When a child responds incorrectly, the round is over. Let the winner remain to compete with another child. You may want to keep track of which child wins the most rounds. In later rounds, you might want to include words on the list that use the long and short vowel sounds of *A* and *I* as well.

Who's-My-Partner? Game   To provide more exercise in discriminating between long and short vowel words, prepare the following word cards: *tub/tube, rod/road, us/use, hop/hope, cub/cube, cot/coat, got/goat, cut/cute.* Distribute the cards and direct the children to find a partner who has a word that is spelled with the same consonants but has a different vowel sound. Ask each pair of children to show their cards to the group and use their long vowel words in a sentence. Encourage children to think of a sentence that uses both the long and short vowel word. (For example: *He put my coat on the cot.*)

Reading   Write the following sentences on the chalkboard.

1. *Luke has a hole in his suit.*
2. *Cole has a cute pet mule.*
3. *Joe may use my flute.*
4. *Sue and June like to hum tunes.*
5. *She left her notes at home.*
6. *The toad hopped on my toe.*
7. *Joan had a ride in my boat.*

For each sentence, call on a child to read the sentence, circle the long *O* words, and underline the long *U* words. Consider appointing a second child as Checker for each sentence to verify that all long *O* and long *U* words have been identified.

Writing   Duplicate the following incomplete sentences or write them on the chalkboard, omitting the clues in parentheses.

1. *Toothpaste comes in a* _____ . (long *U*, begins with *T*)
2. *You should always obey the* _____ . (long *U*, begins with *R*)

3. *The bottom part of your shoe is called a* _____ . (long *O*, begins with *S*)
4. *Joe looked great in his blue* _____ . (long *U*, begins with *S*)
5. *To water the lawn, Mom used a* _____ . (long *O*, begins with *H*)
6. *Pedro rowed his* _____ . (long *O*, begins with *B*)

For each sentence, provide sound clues for the answer and challenge the children to write the word to complete the sentence. You might invite the child who completes the sentence first to read the completed sentence aloud.

Family Involvement Activity   Duplicate the Family Letter on page 92 of this Teacher's Edition. Send it home with the children.

---

34   **Long Vowel Sounds: U, O**

Say the name of the picture in each box. Then write the missing long vowel.

1. b _o_ ne	2. t _u_ be	3. m _u_ le	4. n _o_ se
5. r _o_ pe	6. f _u_ se	7. d _o_ me	8. t _u_ ne
9. c _u_ be	10. g _o_ at	11. r _u_ le	12. t _o_ ad

Read the words that are part of each sentence. Finish the sentence by writing the words from the box in the correct order.

1. June laid the red _tube on the desk_	desk / the / on / tube
2. If Luke lies on his _bed he will doze_	he / doze / bed / will
3. The baby rode home on the back _of a tame goat_	tame / of / goat / a
4. Joe and Sue _will play a tune_	will / tune / a / play
5. No, Tom, you may _not row the boat_	row / boat / the / not

NAME _____

Lesson 13
Long Vowel *E*   (pages 35–36)

Objective   The child will apply the Long Vowel Rule 1, will read words containing long *E* in isolation and within sentences, and will also correctly apply Long Vowel Rule 2.

Long Vowel Rule 1: If one syllable has two vowels, the first vowel is usually long and the second is usually silent.

Long Vowel Rule 2: If a word or a syllable has one vowel, and it comes at the end of the word or syllable, that vowel is usually long.

Teaching Ideas

Listening/Speaking   To present the difference between the short and long vowel sounds of *E*, write the following short vowel words on the chalkboard: *bed, met, set, red, men.* Invite a volunteer to read each word, identify the vowel sound, and explain why the vowel is short. Then write the following long *E* words under the corresponding short *E* words: *bead, meat, seat, read, mean.* Ask a child to read each of the words and tell why the *E* is long. If a child needs guidance, you might ask questions such as the following: *How many vowels do you see? What is the sound of the first vowel? Can you hear the second vowel?*

To introduce long *E* words that follow Long Vowel Rule 2, write the following words on the chalkboard: *we, me, she, begin.* Ask children what vowel sound they hear in each word. Help them identify the sound as long *E*. Then point out that although the sound of *E* is long, these words do not follow the Long Vowel Rule 1. Explain that there is a second long vowel rule and then read Long Vowel Rule 2. Call on volunteers to explain in their own words how each of the words on the chalkboard follows that rule.

Cooperation-Rhyming Game   Consider using rhyming words to offer children more practice in recognizing the long *E* sound. Write the following words on the chalkboard: *meat, need, me.* Divide the children into cooperative groups of three or four. Explain that each group is to work together to make up the longest possible list of rhyming words for each word on the chalkboard. Give the children seven to ten minutes to work on their lists. Then have groups share their lists with each other. You might be able to recognize different categories of winners. (For example, one group may have the largest overall number of rhyming words in all three categories, while a second group has the largest total of words that rhyme with *meat.*) Help the children recognize that some words that rhyme with *me* will follow Long Vowel Rule 2—for example: *he, she, be*—while others follow Long Vowel Rule 1—for example: *see, flea, tea, pea, knee.*

Long Vowel Sound: E   [35]

Long Vowel Rule I
If a syllable or a one-syllable word has two vowels, the first vowel usually has a long sound and the second vowel is silent.

The word **seal** has the long sound of the vowel e. Say the name of the picture in each box. If the name has the long sound of e, circle the picture.

1. seal	2. ten 10	3. beak	4. jeep	5. jet
6. fence	7. beads	8. teeth	9. seat	10. sled
11. beads	12. steps	13. leaf	14. dress	15. sixteen 16
16. eagle	17. street	18. check	19. meat	20. playpen
21. peacock	22. pretzel	23. beaver	24. heel	25. wheelbarrow

The short vowel words in the first column of each box have been changed to long vowel words in the second column. Draw a line to join these words.

1.		2.	
red	need	set	cute
Ben	peep	bed	kite
pep	bean	cut	Pete
bet	read	pet	seat
Ned	beat	kit	bead

3.		4.	
pad	feed	led	mean
met	hide	net	weed
ten	meet	wed	lead
fed	paid	men	beast
hid	teen	best	neat

NAME _____

Long Vowel Sound: E   [36]

Say the name of the picture in each box. Then write the missing vowel.

1. j _e_ ep	2. f _e_ et	3. p _i_ pe	4. b _e_ e
5. t _o_ ad	6. qu _e_ en	7. l _e_ af	8. c _u_ be
9. s _e_ al	10. r _a_ ke	11. s _e_ al	12. b _e_ ads

Read the words that are part of each sentence. Finish the sentence by writing the words from the box in the correct order.

1. The more we read, the more _we like to read_	like read to we
2. The size of the desk top is four _feet by five feet_	feet feet five by
3. The deer got too near the _bees in the trees_	in tree bees the
4. The least we can do is to make Pete _feel at home here_	at here feel home
5. Jean will feed the geese, and Red _will feed the seals_	feed will seals the

NAME _____

30

Lesson 14
Long Vowel Compound Words (page 37)

Objective The child will read words containing two long vowel syllables and will identify each syllable in these words.

Review

Sit-Down Game To give children practice in auditory perception of long and short vowel sounds, prepare the following word cards.

band	camp	gift	fuzz	hunt	doll	lost
end	ate	game	five	life	lift	rude
use	foam	hole	hot	bean	be	bet

Direct the children to stand at their seats. Flash a card and ask the first child to read the word, identify the vowel sound heard in that word, and tell the rule governing it. After a correct response, the child may sit down. Continue using the word cards in the same manner with the remaining children.

Teaching Ideas

Reading/Speaking You might introduce the idea of compound words by reminding the children that they have learned a number of words in which two short vowel words were combined into a single word. Write the following compound words on the chalkboard: *sandbox, windmill, upset*.

Call on a volunteer to read each word, draw a slash between the two small words, and identify the vowel sound in each part. Help the children recognize that both small words use short vowel sounds.

Continue by writing the following long vowel compound word on the chalkboard: *pipeline*. Have the children repeat this word after you as you read it aloud. Then ask if the vowel sound in the word is long or short. When a child answers correctly, challenge the child to come forward and draw a slash between the two long vowel words in the word. Invite the child to call on a classmate to use the compound word in a sentence. Then, continue in the same manner with the following words: *mealtime, homemade, maybe, oatmeal, driveway*.

Where's-the-Rest-of-My-Word? Game Some children may have mistakenly concluded that compound words are made up of either two short vowel words or two long vowel words. To reinforce awareness that compound words can be made up of one short vowel and one long vowel word, play the Where's-the-Rest-of-My-Word Game. Display the following word cards on the chalkboard ledge: *neck, cup, sea, bed, pea, mail, pan*. Then distribute the following word cards to children to use as the second word in the compound: *tie, cake, sick, time, nut, box, cake*. Direct these children to each find a card on the chalkboard ledge that can be combined with the words on their cards to create a compound word. When all the cards have been chosen, let these children each show their cards to the class and read the resulting compound word. Encourage children to use the compound word in a sentence.

Extension

Writing Challenge a child to write a brief story using three to five of the compound words used in the Teaching Ideas activities. You might invite the child to illustrate the story.

Long Vowel Compound Words 37

A compound word is made up of two or more one-syllable words. Circle each one-syllable word in the compound words below.

1. railroad	2. raincoat	3. beehive	4. sailboat	5. maybe	6. lifetime
7. beside	8. teammate	9. homemade	10. oatmeal	11. mealtime	12. seahorse
13. pipeline	14. cupcake	15. lifeboat	16. seacoast	17. hayride	18. fireside
19. necktie	20. subway	21. fireboat	22. rainbow	23. forecast	24. rowboat

Find the compound word in each box to complete the sentence. Circle the word. Then write the word on the line.

1. If you do not have a ___raincoat___ you will get wet.	(raincoat) rainbow mudhole
2. Maybe we can go on a **hayride** at the fair.	homemade (hayride) fireside
3. Tom and his dad ride the **subway** each day.	away (subway) sunset
4. The cab will stop beside the **railroad**	rainbow lifetime (railroad)
5. Lots of red and yellow sails can be seen along the **seacoast**	sandman (seacoast) mailbox
6. As the sun came out after the rain, we saw a **rainbow** in the east.	necktie railway (rainbow)

NAME _____

Unit 5 Consonant Blends

Lesson 15
R Blends (pages 38–39)

Objective The child will associate *r* blends with the sound each represents in words.

A consonant blend consists of two or three consonants that are sounded together in which the sound of each letter can be heard.

Teaching Ideas

Listening You might use the *tr* blend to introduce the concept of consonant blends. Pronounce the following words one at a time: *tree, trick, train, true*. Have the children repeat each word after you. Then ask a volunteer to name the two letters at the beginning of each word. When a child answers correctly, write the words on the chalkboard and invite the child to come forward and circle the *tr* blend. Explain that when two consonants are sounded together, the sound is called a *consonant blend*.

To let the children know that there are many *r* blends, write the following words on the chalkboard: *crab, frog, drum, tree, brake, press, green, grass*. For each, invite a child to read the word and then circle the *r* blend.

How-Many-Words? Game Direct small groups of children to use a specified time period to list as many *r* consonant blend words as possible. Write the following blends on the chalkboard as a reference: *cr, dr, br, fr, gr, pr, tr*. To simplify checking the lists you might suggest children list all the words that use a given blend in a column on a sheet of paper. At the end of the designated time, determine the group that has identified the most words.

Reading Write the following sentences on the chalkboard.

1. *On a hill, a driver must use the brakes.*
2. *The dragonfly ate the green bug.*
3. *Who tried to frame Fred's drawing?*
4. *Are the crab and the frog going to get away?*
5. *The bride and the groom went to breakfast.*
6. *Do you like the yellow fringe on those drapes?*

For each sentence, ask a volunteer to read the sentence and then to circle all the words containing an *r* blend.

Extension

Shopping-List Game To encourage awareness of *r* blend words, invite the child to make out a shopping list of eight things the child would really like to have. Explain that each item on the list must have an *r* blend. Consider offering the child old magazines, catalogs, or advertising inserts to help with ideas for the list.

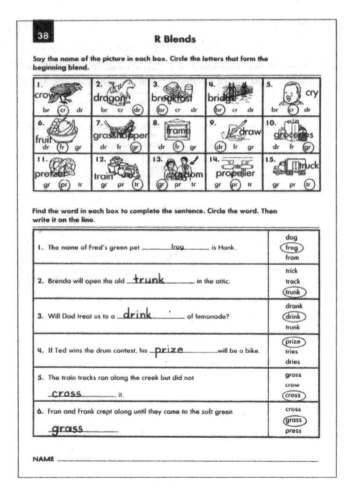

32

Lesson 16
L Blends (pages 40–41)

Objective The child will associate *l* blends with the sound each represents in words.

Review

Writing Review *r* blends in short and long vowel words by arranging the following picture flashcards on the chalkboard ledge: *apron, crib, dress, drum, fruit, grapes, trailer, train, tree.* Call on a volunteer to write the name of each picture above its card on the chalkboard and then to circle the *r* blend in the word.

Teaching Ideas

Listening Introduce *l* blends by contrasting them with *r* blends. Write the following words on the chalkboard: *grow, free, breed, prank.* For each word, invite a volunteer to read the word, write a new word by changing the *r* in the word to *l*, and then read the new word. When all of the words have been changed, point out that the new words all begin with a consonant blend. Invite other children to circle the *l* blend in one of these words and then to use the word in a sentence.

Read each of the following words: *blade, cloud, plan, flag, glad, glue, flat, clock.* For each, invite a volunteer to repeat the word and then to identify the *l* blend.

How-Many-Words? Game Play the How-Many-Words? Game described in Lesson 15 in this unit. Write the following blends on the chalkboard as a reference: *bl, cl, fl, gl, pl.* (Save the word lists for use in the Extension activity that follows.)

Drawing Game Prepare the following word cards: *flame, clock, flag, plant, flower, block, glass, cloud, pliers, playground.* Invite a volunteer to come forward and pick one of the word cards. Have the child draw the item on the chalkboard and invite classmates to identify the *l* blend word that names the picture. Point out that the child who is drawing may not offer clues by speaking but can add to or change the drawing as the guessing occurs. Once the picture is identified, have the child who drew the picture label it and circle the *l* blend. Let the game continue by having the child who guessed the answer choose another word card to draw. You might want to vary the format by establishing teams that compete with each other as in the television game "Win, Lose, or Draw."

Extension

Writing Challenge a child to write three sentences and have each sentence include at least two *l* blend words. You might suggest that the child refer to the word lists generated in the How-Many-Words? Game as a word bank. Challenge the child to use more than the minimum number of *l* blend words in a sentence.

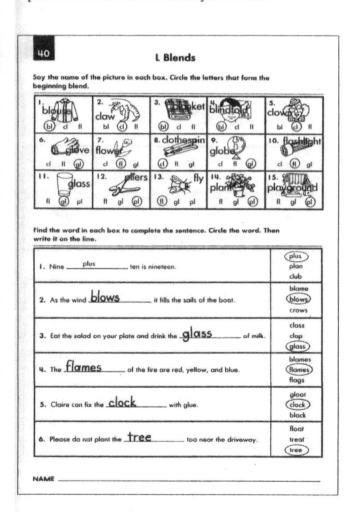

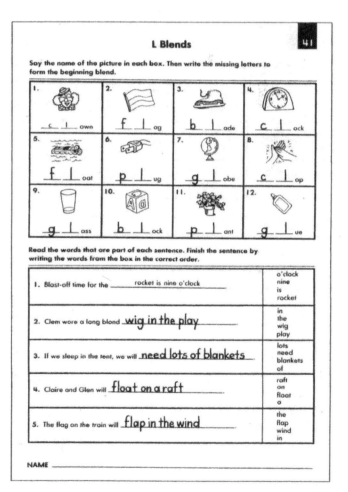

Lesson 17
S Blends (pages 42–43)

Objective The child will associate *s* blends with the sound each represents in words.

Teaching Ideas

Listening As you introduce the *s* blends, you might remind students that a consonant blend may have two or three consonants that blend. Then challenge the children to listen carefully to identify the number of consonant sounds they hear at the beginning of each of the following words: *string, spring, strong, scrape, splat.* For each word, recognize each child who correctly identifies the three consonants that blend and invite the child to write the blend on the chalkboard. You might want to repeat the procedure with the following *s* blends: *spot, sled, skill, swim, stairs, smoke, swim.*

Pantomime Game Play the Pantomime Game by selecting volunteers to perform actions for words containing *s* blends. Encourage the other children to guess the action being pantomimed. You might invite the child who guesses the action to be the next actor. If a child has difficulty thinking of an appropriate word, consider offering the following words for actions that contain an *s* blend: *smiling, swimming, skating, spilling, scrubbing, swinging.*

Speaking/Listening Distribute the following word cards: *stand, snow, smile, spill, sling, splint, straw, scream,* *split, story, sprint.* Have each child in turn read the word on the card, and then invite another child to spell the *s* blend heard at the beginning of the word and to use the word in a sentence. If the listener cannot identify the blend correctly, have the reader show the word card and point to the blend.

Reading Write the following sentences on the chalkboard.

1. *Please paint my swing set green and blue.*
2. *Who spilled my drink on the driveway?*
3. *Stella likes snakes and spiders.*
4. *The class will slide on the slope of the playground.*

Appoint a Speaker and a Scribe for each sentence. Ask the Speaker to read the sentence aloud, and then to name the *s* blend words for the Scribe to circle. Next, have the Speaker identify all other consonant blend words for the Scribe to underline. (Before beginning the activity, you might want to write the words *Speaker* and *Scribe* on the chalkboard and explain them to the children.) Help the children to recognize that both Speaker and Scribe are *s* blend words.

Extension

Shopping-List Game Invite a child to play the Shopping-List Game described in Lesson 15 in this unit, using *s* blend words.

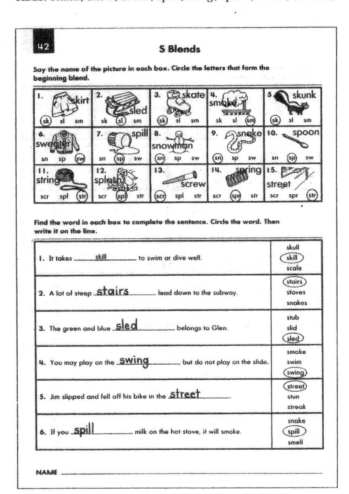

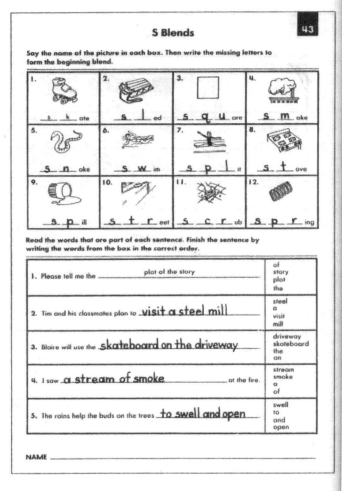

34

Lesson 18

Consonant Digraphs *TH* and *WH* (page 44)

Objective The child will associate the consonant digraphs *th* and *wh* with the sound each represents in words.

Review

How-Many-Words? Game Provide an opportunity to review *s* blend words by grouping children into learning teams to play the How-Many-Words? Game. Write the following list of *s* blends on the chalkboard as a reference: *scr, spl, spr, str, sl, sk, sp, st, sm, sw*. Because an enormous number of *s* blend words occur in English, you may want to extend the time the groups are given to generate their lists.

Teaching Ideas

Listening Write the following words in two rows on the chalkboard: *this, that, them, think, thorn, three*. Invite a volunteer to read the first word and then to identify the sound heard at the beginning of the word. Circle the *th* and point out that the letters *t* and *h* combine to make a new consonant sound. Explain that when a new consonant sound is formed from two consonants in this way, it is called a *consonant*

digraph. Continue by asking other children to read each of the remaining words and circle the consonant digraph.

Speaking You may want to call attention to the difference between the hard and soft sound of the digraph *th*. Have the children hold their hands in front of their mouths as they repeat each row of words after you. They should be able to feel the stronger flow of air that accompanies the soft *th* digraph in *think, thorn,* and *three*.

44

Consonant Digraphs: TH, WH

The word **think** begins with a sound of th. Say the name of the picture in each box. If the name begins with a sound of th, circle the picture.

1. think	2. thumb	3. track	4. thimble	5. three
6. tree	7. trap	8. thorn	9. thirty	10. train
11. throne	12. two	13. thermometer	14. truck	15. thirteen

The word **wheel** begins with the sound of wh. Say the name of the picture in each box. If the name begins with the sound of wh, write wh on the line.

1. wheel wh	2. whistle wh	3. white wh	4. throne	5. thorn
6. whip wh	7. hat	8. wheat wh	9. thumb	10. whale wh
11. horse	12. whiskers wh	13. hand	14. wheelbarrow wh	15. hammer

NAME

35

Lesson 19
Consonant Digraphs *SH* and *CH* (pages 45–48)

Objective The child will identify and name the sounds of the *sh* and *ch* digraphs.

Review

Speaking To review long vowel words, you may wish to write the following sentences on strips of tagboard.

1. *The meat is ready to eat.*
2. *I ate the cake with ice cream.*
3. *We played many games.*
4. *The baby has a smile on her face.*
5. *Mom made green beans for dinner.*
6. *I like to skate on the ice.*
7. *I will have a seat at the table.*
8. *I will read three books.*
9. *We cannot fly our kite in the rain.*
10. *The white puppy has a cold nose.*
11. *We can jump and slide in the snow.*
12. *The wild tiger was in the cage.*

Group the children into pairs. Distribute one sentence strip to each pair. Invite one of the children in each pair to read the sentence aloud. You may ask the other child in each pair to name the long vowel words in the sentence. Repeat this procedure until all the children have read their sentences.

Teaching Ideas

Speaking Write the following words in two columns on the chalkboard: *shadow, relish, washer, fishnet; stretch, armchair, pitcher, chimney.* Invite the children to read each word in column one. Then challenge volunteers to underline the consonant digraph in each word. Reinforce the fact that the consonant digraph in the words in column one is *sh*. Ask the children to use each of the words in a sentence. Repeat the same procedure for the words in column two, reinforcing the fact that the consonant digraph in column two is *ch*.

Listening/Writing Invite each of the children to write the following digraphs across the top of a sheet of paper, forming four column headings. You may want to write the digraphs on the chalkboard in the same fashion: *th, ch, wh, sh.* Explain to the children that you are going to say several words that contain one of the consonant digraphs. Encourage the children to listen carefully for the consonant digraph in each word. Explain that after you say each word, the children should write the word under the appropriate heading on their paper. Say the following words: *trash, wheel, choice, weather, show, kitchen, tooth, wharf.* Ask the children to check their

work by inviting volunteers to write the words that belong with each digraph on the chalkboard. Acknowledge each correct response, providing help with spelling as it is needed.

Write the following sentences on the chalkboard.

1. She saw three shirts on the top shelf.

2. The chief liked to eat cheese.

3. Do you think our wheelbarrow needs a new wheel?

4. When you go shopping, please buy fish and cherries.

Encourage the children to read each of the sentences aloud. Ask the children to circle the words containing a consonant digraph. Challenge the children to identify the consonant digraph in each circled word.

Listening   Say each of the following words: *shopping, sixth, cherries, pitcher, father, fishbowl, whisper, crash, dishes, whale.* After saying a word, ask the children to identify the digraph heard in it and the position of the digraph in the word. (You may need to repeat a word several times.) Encourage the children to use each word in a sentence.

Tongue-Twister Game   Challenge the children to play the Tongue-Twister Game. Write the following sentences on the chalkboard.

1. Shirley and Shelly saw shells near the seashore.

2. Chester and Charlie chased their chum Chuck.

3. Sharon and Sheila shared shoes at the shop.

Ask the children to read each of the sentences aloud as quickly and accurately as possible. (If necessary, explain that the sentences on the chalkboard are called tongue twisters, be-cause so many of the words in each sentence start with the same sound.) If you wish, you may divide the children into two teams. Suggest that the teams create their own set of tongue twisters, providing one for each child on the opposite team. (The tongue twisters can be silly or nonsensical.) Ask the children to record the tongue twisters on strips of tagboard. Invite the children to choose a partner from the opposite team. Ask the partners to exchange tongue twisters. Challenge each child to read the partner's tongue twister as quickly and accurately as possible for the rest of the team.

Consonant Digraphs — 47

Say the name of the picture in each box. Circle the name.

#	Picture	Options
1.	(sheep)	sharp, (sheep), sleep, steep
2.	(3)	these, tree, (three), theme
3.	(chick)	(chicks), checks, shakes, cheeks
4.	(half circle)	width, wheat, whale, (white)
5.	(wheel)	whale, ahead, while, (wheel)
6.	(man face)	(chin), chain, shin, clan
7.	(ship)	shift, thick, (ship), trap
8.	(30)	third, dirty, (thirty), thin
9.	(chain)	chair, (chain), shame, claim
10.	(whip)	wept, (whip), wipe, what
11.	(cherry)	spears, cheery, smear, (cherry)
12.	(moth)	(moth), mitt, math, melt
13.	(fish)	fist, lash, (fish), last
14.	(chair)	tones, thrown, these, (throne)
15.	(crutch)	much, mush, (crutch), catch
16.	(whistle)	thimble, whittle, (whistle), thistle
17.	(thrush)	(thrush), teach, teeth, thrust
18.	(cheer)	sheer, (cheer), sheen, chair
19.	(wishbone)	fishbone, (wishbone), whichever, whenever
20.	(wheat)	when, cheat, (wheat), three
21.	(children)	child, chimney, chill, (children)
22.	(wheelbarrow)	(wheelbarrow), wheel, welcome, which
23.	(chipmunk)	chimp, shipment, champion, (chipmunk)
24.	(shadow)	chatter, shatter, shining, (shadow)

NAME _____

Consonant Digraphs — 48

Read the words that are part of each sentence. Finish the sentence by writing the words from the box in the correct order.

1.	Which child wishes to ___*help with the dishes*___ ?	help, the, with, dishes
2.	The sheep that graze *here have thick coats*	coats, here, thick, have
3.	Carlos has seen a *whale near the beach*	the, near, whale, beach
4.	Tom rests his chin on his *hand when he thinks*	thinks, he, when, hand
5.	May will catch *and Chip will pitch*	Chip, pitch, will, and
6.	Who will whip the cream for the top *of the chocolate cake* ?	the, of, cake, chocolate
7.	When you leave the cabin, please *shut the kitchen door*	door, kitchen, shut, the
8.	The chimpanzee ate a banana from *the dish of fruit*	the, fruit, of, dish
9.	After lunch, we used the wishbone *and made a wish*	and, wish, made, a
10.	Three thin coats of wax will *make a floor shine*	shine, floor, a, make
11.	We can hear the chatter of a *chipmunk in the forest*	the, in, forest, chipmunk

NAME _____

Lesson 20
Y and *W* as Vowels (pages 49–50)

Objective   The child will read words ending in *Y* or *W* by applying the vowel rule appropriate to the words.

Vowel *Y* Rules: IF *Y* is the only vowel at the end of a one-syllable word, it has the long sound of *I*, as in *cry*. If *Y* is the only vowel at the end of a word of more than one syllable, it has the sound of long *E*, as in *baby*.

Vowel *W* Rule: If *W* comes at the end of a word or syllable, it is a vowel, as in the word *snow*.

Review

Listening   Provide the children with two small squares of construction paper or tagboard. Invite the children to write the letter *W* on one square, and the letter *Y* on the second square. Say each of the following words: *yo-yo, yes, yellow, yawn, will, wet, west, wind.* Ask the children to raise the *W* square when they hear a word that starts with *W*, and the *Y* square when they hear a word that starts with *Y*.

Teaching Ideas

Speaking   Write the following words in two columns on the chalkboard: *my, try, sky; bunny, baby, funny.* Invite the children to read each word and say the sound of *Y*. Ask the children to identify those words that have one syllable. Review with them the rule that when *Y* is the only vowel at the end of a one-syllable word, *Y* represents the long *I* sound. You may continue by asking the children to identify those words with more than one syllable. Review with them the rule that when *Y* comes at the end of a word with more than one syllable, it usually represents the long *E* sound.

Listening   Write the following words on the chalkboard: *pry, fly, try, sly, Billy, Bobby, puppy, Sally.* Ask the children to read each word aloud. Challenge the children to listen for the number of syllables in each word. (You may wish to have the children clap out the syllables in each word.) Encourage the children to give, in their own words, the Vowel *Y* Rule governing each of the words.

Writing   Write the following sentences on the chalkboard.

1. *Molly likes to eat a bowl of cereal every day.*
2. *Why did Sally ride her pony in the yard?*
3. *Jimmy spoke softly to the weary puppy.*

Invite volunteers to read each sentence and circle each *Y* or *W* that is a vowel.

Y and W as Vowels — 49

When y and w come at the beginning of a word or syllable, they are consonants.
When y and w come at the end of a word or syllable, they are vowels.

Read each sentence. Underline each y or w that is a consonant. Circle each y or w that is a vowel.

1. Silly Willy will play in the wet clay.
2. Wipe your muddy feet on the mat by the door.
3. Tammy, may we wade in the shallow creek?
4. On the way home we met a stray dog.
5. The snowman that we made last year wore a bow tie.
6. The black crow will try to steal the candy from the sly fox.
7. In the story the white eagle flies up into the sky.
8. Kay will open the yellow drapes and close the window.
9. Tom will plant trees today in the backyard, and his wife will sow grass seed.
10. Can you stay with my baby? He will wake up at ten o'clock and cry for milk.
11. A strong wind can blow the dry sand miles beyond the windmill.

Make a list of all the words from the sentences above in which y and w are silent vowels.

Silent Y Words		Silent W Words	
play	stray	shallow	yellow
clay	Kay	snowman	window
may	today	bow	sow
way	stay	crow	blow

NAME _____

---

50 — **Y as a Vowel**

1. When y is the only vowel at the end of a one-syllable word, it has the long sound of the vowel i.
2. When y comes at the end of a word that has more than one syllable, it usually has the long sound of the vowel e.

Read each word. Write it in the correct column.

by	sly	happy	windy	dry	try
taffy	Molly	silly	fly	lucky	cry

Y has the long sound of i.		Y has the long sound of e.	
by	dry	taffy	silly
sly	try	Molly	windy
fly	cry	happy	lucky

Read the words that are part of each sentence. Finish the sentence by writing the words from the box in the correct order.

1. Hoppy, the bunny, likes to play	with the shy chipmunk	.	the shy with chipmunk
2. Today Sandy and I will	fly to the capital		to capital the fly
3. Why is the grass so green and	the sky so blue	?	so sky blue the
4. Molly is happy to	have a tiny puppy		a have puppy tiny

NAME _____

Lesson 21
Hard and Soft Sounds of C (page 51)

Objective   The child will distinguish between the soft and hard sound of *C* when reading words in isolation or within sentences.

Soft C Rule: If *C* is followed by *E, I*, or *Y*, it usually represents the soft sound of *C*, or the sound of *S*, as in *city*.

Teaching Ideas

Speaking   Write the following words in three columns on the chalkboard: *cabin, comet; cinch, celebrate; juice, cute.* Invite volunteers to read both words in the first column. Ask the children to identify the sound of *C* and the vowel that follows *C* in each word. Reinforce the fact that *C* makes the *K* sound, or the hard sound of *C*, in each of the words in column one. You may continue by asking the children to read each word in column two. Ask the children to identify the sound of *C* in this column of words, and the vowel that follows each word. Reinforce the fact that in column two, *C* makes the sound of *S*, or the soft sound of *C*. Explain to the children that when *C* is followed by *E, I*, or *Y*, it usually has the soft sound of *C*, or the *S*, sound. Challenge the children to read the words in column three. Invite volunteers to explain why *C* has the hard or soft sound.

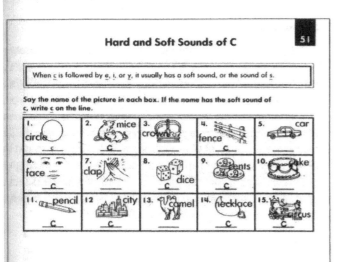

Listening   You may wish to have the children take out a piece of ruled paper and number the lines from *1* to *15*. Explain to the children that you are going to say fifteen words that have either the hard sound of *C* or the soft sound of *C*. Ask the children to identify which sound they hear by printing the letter *K* for the hard sound of *C*, and the letter *S* for the soft sound of *C*, after the appropriate number on their papers. Say the following words, being sure to state the number before each word. (The correct answers are provided for you in parentheses.)

1. cub (K)	*6. fence (S)*	*11. corn (K)*
2. center (S)	*7. face (S)*	*12. cattle (K)*
3. cost (K)	*8. ceiling (S)*	*13. juice (S)*
4. nice (S)	*9. cabin (K)*	*14. cellar(S)*
5. can (K)	*10. city (S)*	*15. candy (K)*

Encourage the children to check their work as you repeat the words and have the children identify the sound of *C*.

Conductor Game   You may wish to challenge the children with the Conductor Game. Write the following words on squares of construction paper or tagboard.

camp	*cup*	*cake*	*cane*	*cube*
coat	*candy*	*catch*	*cent*	*city*
fence	*fireplace*	*pencil*	*price*	*cymbals*

Invite volunteers to arrange their chairs or desks in a row. Ask the child in the first chair of the row to stand behind the child sitting in the second chair. Explain to the children that you are going to flash one of the word cards to the first two children. Tell them that the first child to pronounce the word correctly and explain why *C* has a soft or hard sound will keep the word card. This word card will become the child's "ticket" to move to the child seated in the next chair. Repeat the procedure with each pair of children. Let the child holding the most tickets at the end of the game be the winner. (You may wish to expand the game by preparing more word cards with hard and soft *C*.)

Extension

Writing   Write the following sentences on the chalkboard.

1. *It's a cinch to paint the cabin's ceiling.*
2. *We decided to dance to the music.*
3. *The city celebrated the holiday with a parade.*
4. *Carmen drank juice at the circus.*
5. *My cute canary ate Cindy's cookie.*

Encourage the child to read each sentence. Have the child circle the soft *C* words, and underline the hard *C* words. You may then wish to have the child explain the Soft *C* Rule.

39

Lesson 22
Hard and Soft Sounds of G (page 52)

Objective The child will distinguish between the hard and soft sounds of *G*.

Soft *G* Rule: If *G* is followed by *E, I,* or *Y,* it usually represents the soft sound of *G,* or the sound of *J,* as in *gem.*

Review

Speaking To review the Soft *C* Rule, you may wish to write the following words on the chalkboard: *cent, cell, dance, face, fireplace, space.* Encourage the children to read each word aloud. Have the children explain the Soft *C* Rule.

Teaching Ideas

Listening Write the following columns of words on the chalkboard.

gait	Gene	page
galaxy	gelatin	giant
gossip	gym	budget

Encourage the children to listen for the sound of *G* in the first column of words as you read the words aloud. Explain to them that in the first column of words, *G* has the hard sound of *G*.

Ask the children to listen to the second column of words as you say them aloud. Encourage the children to identify the vowel that comes after the *G* in each word. Explain to the children that when *G* is followed by *E, I,* or *Y,* it usually has the soft sound of *G,* or the *J* sound. Ask the children to read the words in column three. Challenge them to explain why the hard or soft sound of *G* is heard in each word. Encourage the children to explain the Soft *G* Rule.

Speaking Prepare word cards with the following words: *bridge, fudge, giraffe, gym, huge, page, garden, goose, gown, go.* Show the cards, one at a time. Invite volunteers to read a card, state whether the word has the soft or hard sound of *G,* and use the word in a sentence. (You may wish to have each step completed by a different child in order to encourage as much participation as possible.)

Writing You might wish to write the following sentences on the chalkboard.

1. *The gypsy gave a gem to Gail.*
2. *Vegetables are growing in my large garden.*
3. *The grumpy giant gobbled the giblets and gravy.*
4. *The Gingerbread Boy puppet danced on the stage.*
5. *George changed lanes on the bridge.*
6. *The genie gave us a huge golden goose.*

Encourage the children to read each sentence aloud, listening for the hard and soft *G* sounds. Ask the children to circle the soft *G* word, and to underline the hard *G* words. You may then wish to have the children review why the words have a soft or hard *G* by asking them to apply the Soft *G* Rule.

Reteaching

Listening Provide the child with a piece of tagboard or construction paper. Ask the child to make a word card and print the capital letter *G* on one side of the card, and the capital letter *J* on the other side of the card. Say the following words aloud for the child: *huge, game, giant, garden, stage, gate, globe, giraffe, bridge, cage, frog, goat.* Encourage the child to listen for the sound of *G* in each word. Tell the child that if the *G* has the *J* sound, to flip the card so the letter *J* is facing up; and if *G* has the *G* sound, to flip the card so the letter *G* is facing up. You may wish to continue the exercise by giving the child more words with the hard or soft sound of *G*.

52 Hard and Soft Sounds of G

NAME _____

Lesson 23
Soft Sounds of C and G (pages 53–54)

Objective   The child will distinguish between the soft sounds of *C* and *G*.

Teaching Ideas

Writing   Ask the children to divide a piece of paper into four columns with the following headings, which you may also want to write on the chalkboard.

Hard C   Soft C   Hard G   Soft G

Arrange pictures that name the following objects along the chalkboard ledge: *cage, gate, face, stage, gym, gum, cake, fence, city, mice, bridge, giant.* (The pictures may be prepared by the children as part of the lesson, or simple picture flashcards might also be used.) Ask the children to say the name of each picture, paying close attention to the the sound of the letters *C* and *G* in the picture name. Invite volunteers to spell the words that name each picture, while the other children write the words under the appropriate column on their papers. Invite the children to check their work as you list the words spelled under the correct columns on the chalkboard.

Speaking   Write the following sentences on the chalkboard.

1. *Has the giraffe gone through the gate?*
2. *Cindy has a fancy gem in her collection.*
3. *It is nice to sit near a warm fireplace.*
4. *The police officer received a badge.*
5. *The game can be played in the gym .*

Ask the children to identify the soft *C* and soft *G* words. You may then wish to invite volunteers to circle the soft *C* and soft *G* words. Have the children explain why each of the words circled has a soft *C* or soft *G* sound.

Giant-Step Game   Write the following words on small squares of tagboard or construction paper: *ceiling, city, dance, face, fireplace, juice, price, bridge, edge, giraffe, huge, page.* Using masking tape or chalk, place parallel lines on the floor approximately two feet apart, for a distance of twelve feet. Designate one end of the lines as the *Starting Line*, and the opposite end as the *Goal*. Ask one of the children to stand at the Goal with the word cards. Ask two other children to stand at the Starting Line. Direct the child at the Goal to flash a word card and ask the two children at the Starting Line to say the word being shown. The first child to pronounce the word correctly takes a step to the first line. Proceed in the same way until one of the children reaches the Goal. (This child may then become the person who flashes the cards to the next pair of children.) Repeat the procedure until all the children have had a chance to participate.

Family Involvement Activity   Duplicate the Family Letter on page 93 of this Teacher's Edition. Send it home with the children.

---

53 Soft Sounds of C and G

Say the name of the picture in each box. Write the name on the line below.

1. cage	2. gate	3. face	4. stage
5. gym	6. camel	7. gem	8. fence
9. city	10. mice	11. bridge	12. giant

Find the word in each box to complete the sentence. Circle the word. Then write it on the line.

1. The ___prince___ and princess live with the queen.	price / (prince) / prints
2. The ___ice___ on the pond is too thin to skate on.	(ice) / ace / act
3. We had to cross a huge ___bridge___ to go over the river.	badge / brick / (bridge)
4. We must clean the cabin to get rid of the ___mice___ and cockroaches.	nice / (mice) / race
5. When Gene paid, he received twenty cents in ___change___	chicks / chance / (change)

NAME _____

---

54 Soft Sounds of C and G

Read the words that are part of each sentence. Finish the sentence by writing the words from the box in the correct order.

1. Cindy and Grace keep the ___canary in a cage___.	a / in / canary / cage
2. Janice and Bill like to dance ___to the nice music___	music / to / nice / the
3. A puppy must think that a ___giraffe is a giant___	is / giant / a / giraffe
4. The police will help you cross the ___street in the city___	in / city / street / the
5. Nancy cannot decide whether to ___go to the circus___	circus / the / go / to
6. The children like to play dodge ball ___on the city beach___	on / city / the / beach
7. At the Olympic Games, we sat ___near the judges' stand___	the / judges' / near / stand
8. Tracey wore make-up on her ___face for the play___	face / play / the / for
9. Coach Lodge will be ___the new gym teacher___	new / gym / the / teacher
10. While Gene read the story, the class ___sat in a circle___	in / circle / sat / a
11. The gems are on display at the ___entrance to the palace___	palace / the / to / entrance

NAME _____

Lesson 24

AR (page 55)

Objective The child will associate the letters *ar* with the sound they represent in words.

Review

Speaking To review the sound of consonant *R*, you may wish to write the following sentences on the chalkboard.

1. *Ray's ranch is too dry to raise fruit.*
2. *Rita will bring her radio on the train.*
3. *The grass is a deep shade of green.*

Encourage the children to read each sentence aloud, listening for the *R* sound. Challenge the children to identify the words containing the consonant *R* or an *R* blend.

Teaching Ideas

Listening Write the following words on the chalkboard: *car, farm, tart, hard, yard, art.* Encourage the children to read each word aloud. Invite volunteers to underline the *ar* in each word. Explain to the children that when the vowel *A* and the consonant *R* are sounded together, the two letters usually make the sound of *R*. Ask the children to read the words aloud again, listening for the sound of the *ar* in each word.

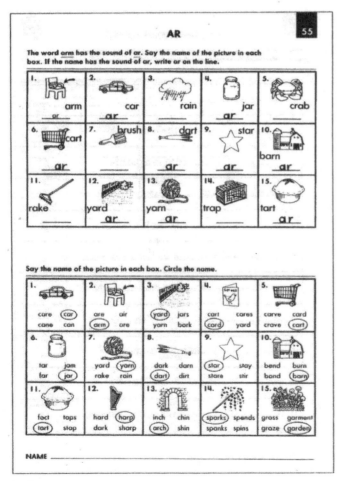

Spelling Game You might ask the children to play the Spelling Game. Invite a volunteer to spell *tar* and to think of a rhyming word. Say that if *tar* is *t-a-r*, then a rhyming word might be the word *far*. Continue by saying the following: *If* t-a-r *is* tar, *and* f-a-r *is* far, *what is* c-a-r? Point out that *c-a-r* is *car*, and continue with the following questions.

1. *If* h-a-r-m *is* harm, *what is* h-a-r-p?
2. *If* l-a-r-k *is* lark, *what is* l-a-r-d?
3. *If* y-a-r-n *is* yarn, *what is* y-a-r-d?
4. *If* s-t-a-r-t *is* start, *what is* s-m-a-r-t?

You may wish to challenge the children to create additional questions. Have the children record the questions on a sheet of paper. Invite volunteers to present their questions to the rest of the class.

Writing Write the following incomplete sentences and words on the chalkboard.

1. *Carlos has a blue _____ .*   arm
2. *Mark has many horses on his _____ .*   car
3. *Marvin fell and broke his _____ .*   farm
4. *Margie grows vegetables in her _____ .*   park
5. *Carmen likes to walk in the _____ .*   garden

Ask the children to read each sentence silently. Tell the children to use the words on the right to complete each sentence. Then invite volunteers to write in the missing word on the chalkboard. Ask the children to read the finished sentences aloud.

Extension

Surprise-Box Game Challenge the child with the Surprise-Box Game. Write the following words on small squares of tagboard or construction paper, and put them in a box: *arch, arm, barn, farm, hard, harm, scarf, spark, start.* Encourage the child to select one of the word cards from the box. Challenge the child to read the word and use it in a sentence. Continue until all the words in the box have been chosen.

Lesson 25

OR (pages 56–58)

Objective The child will associate the letters *or* with the sound they represent in words.

Review

Climb-the-Ladder Game To review the long and short vowel sounds of *O*, you might wish to play the Climb-the-Ladder Game. Draw a ladder on the chalkboard or on a large piece of tagboard. Write one of the following words on each rung of the ladder: *hot, road, oats, no, pot, Joe, rock, top, hole*. Encourage the children to *"climb the ladder"* by beginning at the bottom rung, reading the word on that rung, and identifying its vowel sound. Have the children continue in the same fashion until they have reached the top of the ladder. You may then wish to change the words on the ladder and use the following words: *roast, dock, mop, so, ox, lock, toad, oak, toe*. Encourage the children to climb the ladder again.

Teaching Ideas

Listening Write the following words on the chalkboard: *corn, born, cork, storm, horn, horse, thorn*. Ask the children to read each word aloud. Invite volunteers to circle the *or* in each word. Explain to the children that when the *O*

and *R* are sounded together, the two letters usually make the sound of *or*. Have the children read each word again, listening for the sound of *or*.

Spelling Game You might ask the children to play the Spelling Game, as described in Lesson 24 in this unit, using the following questions.

1. If c-o-r-n *is* corn, *what is* c-o-r-k?
2. If p-o-r-c-h *is* porch, *what is* t-o-r-c-h?
3. If s-t-o-r-k *is* stork, *what is* f-o-r-k?
4. If p-o-r-k *is* pork, *what is* p-o-r-t?

To expand the game you may want to encourage the children to make up more questions that could be presented to the rest of the class.

Catch-Me-If-You-Can Game Another approach is to play this version of the Catch-Me-If-You-Can Game. Print the following words on small squares of tagboard or construction paper.

arch	garden	scarf	spark	short
scorch	storm	start	cars	horse
torch	cord	carton	porch	dark

Divide the children into two teams, forming two straight lines. Flash one of the word cards at the first two children on each team. Ask the children to call out the vowel sound on the word card as quickly as possible. Award a point to the first child to answer correctly. Have both children stand at the end of the correct respondent's team line. Continue the game as described until one team line is eliminated or until each child has

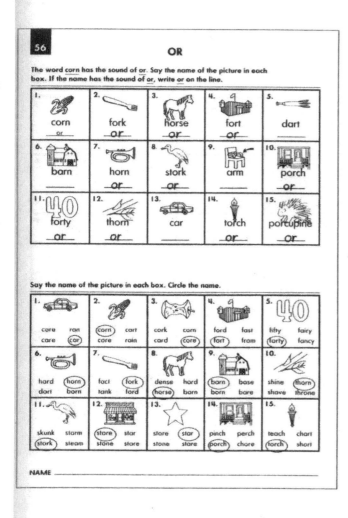

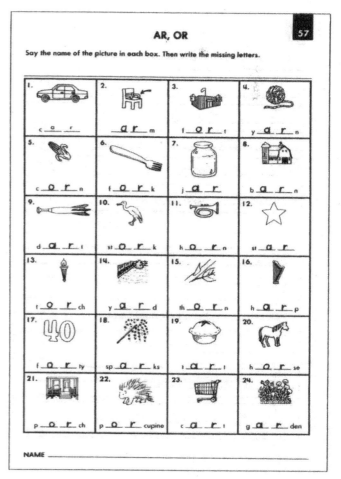

43

had at least one turn. For further reinforcement, you might have the child who gives the correct response write the word on the chalkboard.

Writing   Write the following incomplete sentences and words on the chalkboard.

1. *To the left of my plate is my*

   _____ .   fort   fork

2. *Lori ate her apple, even the*

   _____ .   core   corn

3. *Norm pricked his arm on that*

   _____ .   horn   thorn

4. *Nora wants to ride my*

   _____ .   horse   hornet

5. *Aaron drives a* _____ *car.*   storms   sports

Ask the children to take out a piece of paper and a pencil. Encourage them to read each sentence and write the word that completes each sentence on their papers. Invite volunteers to circle the word that completes each sentence on the chalkboard, while the children check their own work at their desks. You may then wish to have the children read the sentences aloud, using the words that have been circled.

Extension

Writing   Prepare a worksheet for the child by writing the following scrambled words on a piece of paper: *rahm,* *kard, hesor, norhet, storh, denrag, char, chotr.* Before presenting the child with the worksheet, write the following words on the chalkboard: *arch, dark, garden, harm, hornet, horse, short, torch.* Explain to the child that the worksheet has the same words on it that are on the chalkboard, except that the letters on the worksheet have been scrambled. Challenge the child to unscramble the words on the worksheet and to write the correct spelling of the word next to its scrambled version. Remind the child that all the scrambled words are also listed correctly spelled on the chalkboard. Have the child pronounce each word and say if the word has an *ar* or an *or* sound.

58	AR, OR

Find the word in each box to complete the sentence. Circle the word. Then write it on the line.

1. Norman tied the parcel with a strong ____cord____ .	card / (cord) / cork
2. The target for the space probe is ____Mars____ .	Marty / Mrs. / (Mars)
3. We can pack sandwiches for the picnic in this ____carton____ .	carpet / (carton) / arctic
4. Please send these ____garments____ to the City Dress Shop.	gardens / (garments) / parsnips
5. The ____horse____ reared up and upset the fruit cart.	horns / harsh / (horse)

Read the words that are part of each sentence. Finish the sentence by writing the words from the box in the correct order.

1. It is a nice morning to ____start on a trip____	trip / on / a / start
2. Marty can use his ____snorkel in swimming class____	class / swimming / snorkel / in
3. Marta stored the ____corn on the porch____	the / porch / on / corn
4. The ship came into port with ____a load of cars____	a / cars / of / load
5. We will bring parsley from the ____market for the salad____	the / for / market / salad

NAME _____

44

Lesson 26
IR, UR, and ER (pages 59–60)

Objective The child will read and identify the sounds of *ir, ur,* and *er.*

Teaching Ideas

Listening Write the following words on the chalkboard: *urn, curl, churn, purr.* Have the children read each of the words aloud, listening for the *ur* in each word. Invite one of the children to underline the *ur* in each word. Explain to the children that when *U* and *R* are sounded together, the two letters usually make the sound of *ur.*

Follow the same procedure to develop the *ir* and *er* vowel sounds. You may want to use the following *ir* and *er* words: *birth, shirt, dirty, flirt; stern, fern, herd, germ.*

Speaking Point out to the children that the sounds of *ur, ir,* and *er* are very similar. Encourage the children to name more words that have the *ur, ir,* or *er* sound. Record the children's suggestions on the chalkboard. Invite volunteers, in turn, to underline the *ur, ir,* and *er* in each word.

Writing Write the following sentences on the chalkboard.

1. *The dark birds nest in the church tower.*
2. *My race car won first prize in the derby.*
3. *Carl burned his finger on the torch.*
4. *The girl was in a hurry to mail her letter.*
5. *Are Mom and Dad planting the fir tree?*

Have each child write the following headings across the top of a piece of paper: *ir, ur, er.* (You may also want to write the headings on the chalkboard.) Ask the children to read each sentence silently. Encourage the children to find the words in each sentence that have *ir, ur,* or *er.* Have the children write the words under the appropriate columns on their paper. Permit the children to check their work by inviting volunteers to write the answers on the chalkboard. Encourage children to identify the *ar* and *or* words, as well.

Giant-Step Game Print the following words on small squares of construction paper or tagboard.

bark	arm	jar	cord	form	morning
church	curl	letter	spider	thirty	squirm
surprise	hammer				

Play the Giant-Step Game, as explained in Lesson 23, using these word cards.

Reteaching

Beat-the-Card Game Prepare a stack of word cards using the following words: *derby, curve, dirt, herd, hurry, iceberg, mermaid, perfect, thirty.* Invite the child to sit or stand in front of you. Flash the first word card in front of the child and ask the child to spell the vowel sound heard. If the child responds correctly, give the word card to the child. If the child responds incorrectly, keep the word card. Continue in the same manner until the child has won all the word cards.

59

IR, UR, ER

The word *bird* has the sound of *ir.* The letters *ir, ur,* and *er* have the same sound. Say the name of the picture in each box. Circle the name.

1. (bird) bride Burt burst	2. shirt short (skirt) start	3. thirsty (thirty) thirteen thrifty	4. far fin for (fir)
5. fair (fur) from rut	6. spar spore (spur) spare	7. burn press born (purse)	8. curb chore (church) curl
9. farm firm form (fern)	10. hard bird (herd) bead	11. (rocker) racket soccer rocket	12. pork (pitcher) park patches
13. short slant spite (shirt)	14. giraffe (geranium) girl gingerbread	15. gorge gull curl (girl)	16. barbers (rubbers) borders robbers
17. (turkey) turnip tricky parsnip	18. zebra (zipper) bronze sipper	19. forty (thirteen) churns thirty	20. seaman icebox iceman (iceberg)
21. (marching) morning (mermaid) sunset	22. squirt (squirrel) squint squeeze	23. spark spend speak (spider)	24. termite (turtle) tremble turkey

NAME _____

60

AR, ER, IR, OR, UR

Find the word in each box to complete the sentence. Circle the word. Then write it on the line.

1. You need to leave a margin on your _____ paper _____	payer (paper) polar
2. The narrow street was **dirty** and deserted.	story hurry (dirty)
3. We live in a **large** city that has big skyscrapers.	furry (large) darts
4. A **hurricane** is a much larger storm than a tornado.	(hurricane) September carpenter
5. In a city, you may **never** see birds like the thrush.	serve nerve (never)

Read the words that are part of each sentence. Finish the sentence by writing the words from the box in the correct order.

1. The doctor had to pull the **thorn from Bob's finger**	finger from Bob's thorn
2. In the fall, many **farmers harvest their crops**	their harvest farmers crops
3. A bow and arrow **are used in archery**	used are archery in
4. Marta received a parcel in the **mail for her birthday**	mail her birthday for
5. March is the third month of the year, and **the start of spring**	the spring of start
6. On Saturday, Dad picked parsnips **and roasted a turkey**	roasted and a turkey

NAME _____

45

Lesson 27
Vowel Digraph OO (pages 61–64)

Objective The child will distinguish between the two sounds of the vowel digraph *oo*, as heard in *moon* and in *book*.

A vowel digraph is a double vowel that does not follow Long Vowel Rule 1.

Review

Speaking To review Long Vowel Rule 1, you may wish to list the following words on the chalkboard.

glue	tried	stray	bowl
street	yeast	cake	teach
seacoast	railway	cheeks	throat

For each, ask a child to read the word aloud and to identify the vowel sound. (For those words that have two syllables, encourage the children to identify the vowel sound in each part.) Challenge the children to give, in their own words, the vowel rule as it applies to each word.

Teaching Ideas

Listening Write the following words on the chalkboard: *zoo, boots, goose, rooster, broom, spoon, tooth, moon*. Encourage the children to listen for the sound of *oo* as you read each word. Invite a volunteer to underline the *oo* in each word. Explain to the children that because the *oo* in each of these words does not follow Long Vowel Rule 1, *oo* is called a *vowel digraph*. Encourage the children to repeat each word after you and to listen for the vowel digraph in each word.

Next, write the following words on the chalkboard: *book, cook, brook, woods, stood, hood, hook, good*. Have the children repeat each of these words as you say them aloud and encourage them to listen for the new sound of *oo*. Invite a volunteer to underline the *oo* in each word. Explain to the children that the *oo* in these words is also the vowel digraph *oo*. Tell the children that the *oo* digraph can have two sounds: the sound heard in *moon* and the sound heard in *book*.

Speaking Write the following columns of words on the chalkboard or duplicate a copy for each child.

book	cook	cool	boots
hook	nook	took	books
moon	pool	foot	stool
wood	hood	good	broom

Invite volunteers, in turn, to read each column of words. Encourage correct pronunciation. Remind the children that

---

Vowel Digraph Sound: OO 61

A vowel digraph is a double vowel that does not follow Long Vowel Rule 1.

The word zoo has one sound of the vowel digraph oo. Say the name of the picture in each box. Circle each picture with a name that has the sound of oo, as in zoo.

Say the name of the picture in each box. Circle the name.

---

62 **Vowel Digraph Sound: OO**

Find the word in each box to complete the sentence. Circle the word. Then write it on the line.

1. The __raccoon__ raids garbage cans.
2. While Charles sits by the pool, he sips a __cool__ drink.
3. Turnips and carrots are roots that we use for __food__.
4. Did you see the rooster land outside the window of my __room__?

Read the words that are part of each sentence. Finish the sentence by writing the words from the box in the correct order.

1. The baby ate his food __with a spoon__
2. Brett goes home from school for __lunch at noon__
3. It did not hurt when the dentist pulled __his loose tooth__
4. You may choose the swimming pool __or the lagoon__ as the place for the party.
5. When the __moon is full__, you can see shadows.
6. Our class will go to the city to __visit the zoo__

NAME _____

because the vowel digraph *oo* does not follow Long Vowel Rule 1, it can have two different sounds. You may wish to ask volunteers, in turn, to write sentences containing each of the words in a column on the chalkboard.

Team-Rhyming Game Write the word *moon* on the chalkboard. Divide the children into two teams. Ask the first player on team one to name a word that rhymes with *moon*. If the response is correct, have the player go to the end of that team's line. Then give the first player on team two an opportunity to think of another word that rhymes with *moon*. Alternate between the two teams until the players cannot think of any more words that rhyme with *moon*. Continue the game by writing the word *book* on the chalkboard. Play the game using the same procedure. (To help the children remember which words have been used, you may want to record each response on the chalkboard.)

Extension

Art Provide the child with a large piece of newsprint or white construction paper, crayons, markers, or paints. Ask the child to think of words containing the vowel digraph *oo* that name things that might be found outdoors, such as the following: *goose, zoo, rooster, moon, roof, raccoon, lagoon*. Record the child's suggestions on the chalkboard. Encourage the child to draw an outdoor scene, illustrating some of the words listed on the chalkboard.

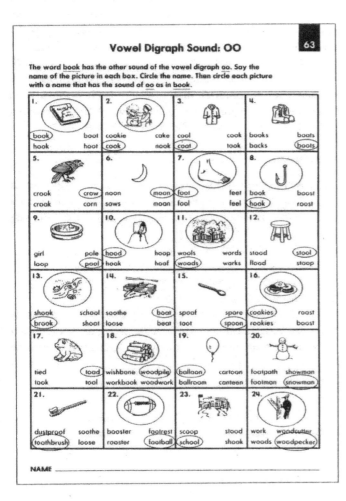

Lesson 28
Vowel Digraph *EA*   (page 65)

Objective   The child will distinguish between the two sounds of the double vowel *ea*.

Review

Climb-the-Ladder Game   To practice recognition of vowel digraph *oo* and its sounds, invite the children to play Climb the Ladder, as described in Lesson 25. You may wish to write the following words on each ladder rung.

stood	*cookie*	*cool*	*wool*
school	*room*	*woodpile*	*rookies*
boost	*balloon*	*football*	*toothbrush*

Teaching Ideas

Listening   Write the following words in two columns on the chalkboard: *beach, team, speak, clean; bread, head, thread, feather.* Encourage the children to listen to the words in column one as you read them aloud. Ask the children to identify the vowel sound represented by double vowel *ea*. Emphasize that the vowel sound *ea* represents in each word is the long sound of vowel *E*. Review with the children Long Vowel Rule 1. Invite volunteers to explain how Long Vowel Rule 1 applies to the words in column one.

Continue by saying the words in column two. Encourage the children to listen for the vowel sound represented by double vowel *ea* in each of the words in column two. Ask the children to identify the vowel sound *ea* represents in each word. Emphasize that the vowel sound *ea* represents in each word is the short sound of vowel *E*. Explain to the children that when *ea* does not follow Long Vowel Rule 1, it is considered irregular. Encourage the children to read each of the words in column two again. You may then wish to invite volunteers, in turn, to underline *ea* in each word to reinforce recognition of the short *E* sound.

Spelling Game   You may wish to play the Spelling Game. Invite a volunteer to spell *bread* and to think of a rhyming word. Point out that if *bread* is b-r-e-a-d, then a rhyming word might be *thread*. Continue using the following questions.

1. If l-e-a-t-h-e-r *is* leather, *what is* f-e-a-t-h-e-r?
2. If f-e-a-t-h-e-r *is* feather, *what is* w-e-a-t-h-e-r?
3. If t-r-e-a-s-u-r-e *is* treasure, *what is* m-e-a-s-u-r-e?
4. If m-e-a-s-u-r-e *is* measure, *what is* p-l-e-a-s-u-r-e?

Writing   Write the following sentences on the chalkboard.

1. Stormy weather threatens our picnic.
2. To weave a sweater, Jean needs beads and thread.
3. For breakfast I spread peanut butter on bread.
4. Having good health is greater than owning many treasures.

For each, have a child read the sentence and underline each word containing double vowel *ea*. Ask each child to select another child to trace the *ea* in each underlined word and to give the vowel sound *ea* makes.

Speaking   Write the following words on the chalkboard: *beads, bread, team, feather, leather.* Ask the children to repeat each word aloud after you. For each word, invite a volunteer to explain whether Long Vowel Rule 1 is used and challenge the child to use the word in a sentence.

Extension

Art   Provide the child with small squares of tagboard or construction paper and crayons or markers. Invite the child to make a personal set of *ea* word cards for the following words.

beads	*bread*	*team*	*feather*
thread	*beaver*	*leaf*	*seal*
treasure	*weapon*	*breakfast*	*deal*
peach	*eagle*	*teapot*	*head*

Have the child write one of the words at the top of each of the squares. Ask the child to illustrate the word, using crayons or markers. Continue until all the words have been illustrated. You may also wish to challenge the child to read each of the word cards aloud.

Vowel Digraph Sound: EA   65

The word bread has the sound of the vowel digraph *ea*. Read each word below. Write the word in the first column if the *ea* follows Long Vowel Rule 1. Write the word in the second column if the *ea* has the vowel sound you hear in bread.

head	treasure	beak	health	weather
seat	weapon	sweater	dream	cleanser
beads	peasant	seal	teammate	headline
feather	beaver	breakfast	eagle	teapot
thread	peach	leaf	threaten	peacock
	dread	oatmeal	peanut	

beads	head
seat	feather
peanut	thread
beaver	treasure
peach	weapon
peacock	peasant
beak	sweater
seal	breakfast
leaf	dread
dream	health
teammate	threaten
eagle	weather
oatmeal	cleanser
teapot	headline

NAME _____

48

Lesson 29
Vowel Digraphs *AU, AW,* and *EI* (page 66)

Objective The child will identify the vowel digraphs *au*, *aw*, and *ei*.

Review

Speaking To practice recognition of compound words, write the following words on the chalkboard: *woodwork, oatmeal, breakfast, dustpan.* Ask the children to repeat each word after you. For each, invite a volunteer to draw a circle around each syllable and to use the word in a sentence.

Teaching Ideas

Listening Write the following columns of words on the chalkboard.

paw	fawn	hawk	crawl
Paul	sauce	fault	author

Read each word aloud, encouraging the children to listen for the vowel sound in each word. Point out that *au* and *aw* have the same sound in all of the words. Explain to the children that *au* and *aw* have the same sound because they are irregular double vowels and do not follow Long Vowel Rule 1. (If necessary, review Long Vowel Rule 1 with the children.) Tell the children that *au* and *aw* are vowel digraphs. Invite volunteers, in turn, to underline the *au* or *aw* digraph in each word.

Speaking Add the following words to the list on the chalkboard: *auto, awning, dawn, fawn, haul, hawk, straw, yawn.* For each, ask a child to read the word aloud and to trace the vowel digraph using a piece of chalk or a finger. You may also wish to challenge each child to use the word in a sentence.

Writing Write the following columns of words on the chalkboard.

Keith	seize	ceiling
veil	reins	eight

Ask the children to listen to each column of words as you read them aloud. Encourage the children to listen carefully for the vowel sound represented by the *ei* in each word. Invite volunteers to write the vowel sound they hear next to each word in the columns. Emphasize that *ei* represents the long sound of *E* in the first word in each column and the long sound *A* in the second word in each column. Explain that when *ei* represents the long sound of *A*, it is an irregular double vowel because it does not follow Long Vowel Rule 1. Emphasize that *ei* is a vowel digraph. You may then wish to have the children write a sentence for each word at their desks, or on the chalkboard. Encourage the children to share their sentences with the rest of the class.

Speaking Write the following words on the chalkboard: *eighty, neighbor, freight, reindeer.* For each, have a child read the word, and challenge the child to use the word in a sentence.

Extension

Listening Write the following words on the chalkboard: *saw, laundry, lawyer, neighbor.* Encourage the child to read each word. Explain to the child that you are going to read some sentences but that you will be leaving out the last word in each sentence. Challenge the child to use one of the words on the chalkboard to complete each of the following sentences.

1. *Tim just bought a new _____ .*
2. *Jane is my next door _____ .*
3. *Dave just became a _____ .*
4. *Today, I will do my _____ .*

Remind the child to use context clues to identify the correct missing words.

66 **Vowel Digraphs Sounds: AU, AW, EI**

The vowel digraph au in auto and the vowel digraph aw in hawk have the same sound. Say the name of the picture in each box. Circle each picture with a name that has the sound of au and aw.

The word eight has the sound of the vowel digraph ei. Read each word below. Write the word in the first column if the ei follows Long Vowel Rule 1. Write the word in the second column if the ei has the vowel sound you hear in eight.

eighty   reins   ceiling   seize   neither   Keith
receive   freight   veil   Sheila   weight   reindeer

receive	eighty
ceiling	reins
seize	freight
Sheila	veil
neither	weight
Keith	reindeer

NAME _____

49

Lesson 30
Vowel Digraphs (pages 67–69)

Objective The child will associate the vowel digraphs *oo, ea, au, aw,* and *ei* with the sound that each digraph represents.

Review

Speaking To recall Vowel *Y* Rules, you may wish to prepare cards for the following words or list the words on the chalkboard: *cry, fly, my, Billy, dolly, happy, pony.* For each, have a child read the word and name the *Y* vowel sound. Challenge each child to give the rule that governs the *Y* and to use the word in a sentence.

Teaching Ideas

Writing Write the following headings on the chalkboard and have each child copy them across the top of a piece of paper: *oo, ea, au, aw, ei.* Explain to the children that you are going to read a list of words containing the vowel digraphs listed on the chalkboard. Slowly read the following words to the children.

book	feather	eight	awning
Paul	reins	cook	leather
dawn	pause	wood	weight
thread	claw	faucet	shawl

Tell the children to listen to each word and to write the word under the appropriate heading on their papers. Invite volunteers to write the words under the correct headings on the chalkboard and encourage the other children to check their work at their desks.

Speaking Write the following words on the chalkboard.

broom	food	pool	foot	hood
wood	bread	head	weather	auto
Paul	straw	yawn	laundry	hawk

Pronounce each word and encourage the children to listen for the vowel digraph. Invite volunteers, in turn, to circle the vowel digraph in each word and to use each word in a sentence.

Giant-Step Game Play the Giant-Step Game, as described in Lesson 23, using the following word cards.

food	pool	spoon	book
bread	feather	spread	weather
draw	dawn	pause	took

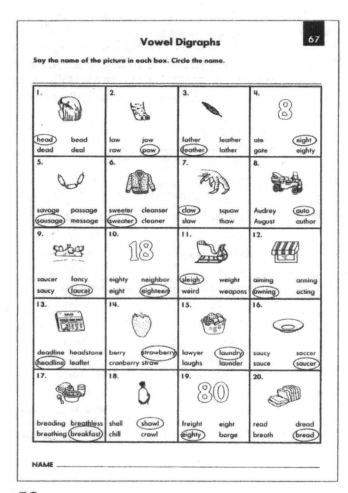

Digraph-Derby Game Write the following columns of incomplete words on the chalkboard. (The complete word is provided in parentheses.)

f __ ther (feather)	r __ ndeer (reindeer)
b __ k (book)	l __ ndry (laundry)
t __ l (tool)	sp __ n (spoon)
bec __ se (because)	w __ l (wool)
y __ n (yarn)	l __ yer (lawyer)
__ ght (eight)	h __ vy (heavy)

Divide the children into two teams. Assign a column from the chalkboard to each team. Tell the teams that each word in their column is missing a vowel digraph. Have the first player on each team go to the chalkboard and write the appropriate digraph in the empty spaces for the first word in that team's column. (You may wish to list the vowel digraphs on the chalkboard if the children have difficulty figuring out the words.) The player must then read the word correctly. If a player cannot complete the task appropriately, let the next player on that team continue with the same word. Continue the game in this manner, until one team completes its column first. To provide an opportunity for each child to participate, you might erase the responses and have the teams switch columns. Repeat the game with the new assignments. The team with the most points at the end of the game wins.

Reteaching

Tactile Write the following sentences on the chalkboard.

1. *The hawk uses its claws to seize food.*
2. *Paul cut the wood with a saw.*
3. *The weight of the bread is marked on the package.*
4. *A reindeer can pull the sled.*
5. *There is a zoo near our school.*
6. *The weather is nice in August.*

Invite the child to read each sentence aloud. Have the child circle the words containing a vowel digraph. Ask the child to trace the vowel digraphs, using either a brightly colored piece of chalk or a finger. Encourage the child to say the words again and to listen for the vowel digraph in each word. (You might invite the child to illustrate one of the sentences.)

Vowel Digraphs 69

Play Tic-Tac-Toe. Draw a line through the three pictures in a row that have the same vowel digraph sound.

1.

sweater	bread	beads
peach	head	peas
beaver	leaf	thread

2.

faucet	fawn	wheat
raccoon	shawl	spider
laundry	awning	seal

3.

moon	book	boots
woods	zoo	foot
cookies	football	woodpecker

4.

hood	tools	raccoon
school	goose	woodpile
rooster	hook	stool

NAME _____

Lesson 31
Diphthongs *OW* and *OU* (pages 70–72)

Objective   The child will associate the diphthongs *ow* and *ou* with the sounds they represent and will read *ow* and *ou* words appearing in isolation and in sentences.

A diphthong consists of two vowels blended together to form one sound.

Review

Reading/Drawing   To practice recognition of the vowel digraphs, you may wish to place the following word cards on the chalkboard ledge: *balloon, thread, book, cookies, football, moon, rooster, bread, broom, spoon*. Point to each word card, encouraging the children to read the word aloud. Invite volunteers to draw pictures on the chalkboard illustrating the words. Then have them each write the word under the appropriate picture.

Listening/Drawing   To expand the activity, you might ask the children to write the following words as you say them aloud: *eight, straw, auto, veil, faucet*. Encourage the children

to draw pictures for each of the words as they did for the words displayed on word cards.

Teaching Ideas

Listening   Display picture flashcards for *doughnuts* and *snowman* and ask the children to name the words they represent. Write the words in a row on the chalkboard as the children name them. Encourage volunteers to identify the vowel sounds in each word and to explain the vowel rule that governs each syllable. Then present the picture flashcards for *clown* and *mouth* and ask the children to name the words they represent. Write the words in a second row on the chalkboard as the children name them. Invite volunteers to identify the vowel sound in each word and to circle the vowels on the chalkboard. Point out that the *ow* in clown and the *ou* in mouth have the same sound. Explain that when two vowels blend together to make one sound, it is called a diphthong.

Spelling Game   Challenge the children with the Spelling Game. Encourage the children to listen carefully for spelling clues as you ask them questions such as the following about words with *ow* and *ou* diphthongs.

If o-w sounds like ow, *how would you spell* plow?
If o-u sounds like ow, *how would you spell* out?

Continue the game using the following words.

ow: plow, sow, crowd, now, growl, howl, towel, cow

ou: out, mouth, loud, mound, sound, found, round

You might wish to challenge the children to create additional questions.

Speaking To reinforce the activity, you may wish to write the following words on the chalkboard and encourage the children to read each word aloud: *hound, sound, round, clown, cow, brown*. Then ask the children to choose from these words to complete sentences you say. You may want to use the following sentences.

1. A hunting dog is sometimes called a _____ . (hound)
2. The color of chocolate is _____ . (brown)
3. The bell made a loud, ringing _____ . (sound)
4. The shape of a ball is _____ . (round)
5. Bill's brown _____ gives lots of milk. (cow)
6. The circus _____ made the people laugh. (clown)

Extension

Writing Write the following words on the chalkboard or duplicate them on paper: *owl, mouse, house, shower, yellow, clown, dough, crowd, bowl, downtown, flour*. Invite the child to circle the words with diphthongs and to write sentences using those words on a sheet of paper. You may want to caution the child that not every *ow* or *ou* combination in a word is a diphthong.

---

72 **Diphthong Sounds: OW, OU**

Find the word in each box to complete the sentence. Circle the word. Then write it on the line.

1. A dark ___cloud___ crossed the moon.	(cloud) / clown / proud
2. Paul found an arrowhead near a big __mound__ of dirt.	mount / (mound) / sound
3. Now you may measure the __flour__ and make the bread.	power / (flour) / flows
4. We are __proud__ to be good citizens of our town.	ground / prowl / (proud)

Read the words that are part of each sentence. Finish the sentence by writing the words from the box in the correct order.

1. The trip downtown ___took about an hour___	an / hour / took / about
2. A dog will keep prowlers __away from the house__	from / away / house / the
3. Will the airport allow visitors __in the control tower__ ?	control / in / tower / the
4. Joan saw eight cows and three __horses in the meadow__	the / in / meadow / horses
5. The hot sun melts the __snow on the mountains__ and causes spring floods.	snow / the / mountains / on
6. We will take our own towels __down to the pool__	to / pool / the / down

NAME _____

Lesson 32
Diphthongs *OY, OI,* and *EW*   (page 73)

Objective   The child will identify the sounds of the diphthongs *oy, oi,* and *ew* and will read *oy, oi,* and *ew* words appearing in isolation and in sentences.

Review

Writing   To help the children review the *ou* and *ow* diphthongs, you may wish to write the following key words in a row on the chalkboard: *how, down, pound, house.* Point to the first key word and invite a volunteer to read it aloud. Encourage the children to form new words by changing the beginning consonant to another consonant or a blend. Children might suggest words such as the following: *bow, cow, now, plow.* Write each new word under the key word on the chalkboard and encourage a volunteer to use the new word in a sentence. Continue the review by repeating the activity with each of the other key words.

Teaching Ideas

Listening   Write *boy* and *coin* on the chalkboard and underline the diphthong in each. Encourage the children to say the words aloud and to listen for the vowel sounds. Point out

that the *oi* and the *oy* have the same vowel sound. Explain that *oy* and *oi* are called diphthongs because they join together to form a new sound.

Next, you may display a newspaper at the front of the classroom and ask the children to identify it. As the children say the word *newspaper,* write it on the chalkboard and underline the *ew* diphthong. Invite the children to repeat the *ew* sound in the word. Point out that these vowels are joined to make one sound, called a diphthong.

Speaking   Write the following phrases on sentence strips and arrange them facedown on the desk.

the new screwdriver	*oily coils*
mouse in the house	*avoid sewers*
a few noisemakers	*newspaper blew*
county boy scouts	*Moira's jewelry*

Invite volunteers to choose a sentence strip, read it to the other children, and write the phrase on the chalkboard. Then encourage the children to underline the diphthongs and to use the phrases in sentences. You may wish to have the children say the sentences aloud or write them on the chalkboard. (Save the sentence strips for the Extension activity that follows.)

Extension

Art   Encourage the child to choose one of the sentence strips from the previous activity. Have the child write a sentence that includes the phrase across the top of a sheet of drawing paper. Provide crayons, and invite the child to create an illustration that corresponds with the sentence.

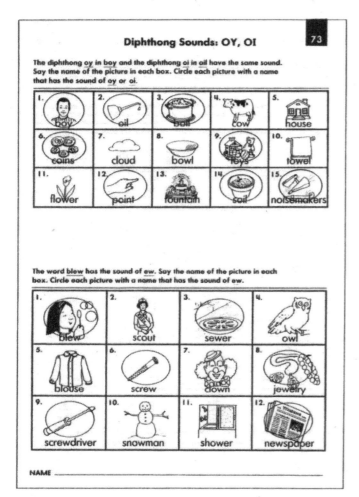

Lesson 33
Diphthong Review (pages 74–76)

Objective The child will distinguish between the sounds of the diphthongs *ou, ow, oy, oi,* and *ew* and will read words containing these diphthongs.

Review

Rhyming Game To review the sound of diphthongs and vowel diagraphs, and the elements of rhymes, you might present the following riddles and invite volunteers to supply the correct rhyming words.

1. *It rhymes with* toy *and begins with* j. *(joy)*
2. *It rhymes with* proud *and begins with* cl. *(cloud)*
3. *It rhymes with* moon *and begins with* sp. *(spoon)*
4. *It rhymes with* eight *and begins with* fr. *(freight)*
5. *It rhymes with* book *and begins with* sh. *(shook)*
6. *It rhymes with* head *and begins with* thr. *(thread)*
7. *It rhymes with* paw *and begins with* str. *(straw)*
8. *It rhymes with* down *and begins with* cl. *(clown)*

Teaching Ideas

Writing Write the following diphthongs in a row on the chalkboard: *ou, ow, oy, oi, ew.* Then write the following incomplete words on the chalkboard.

t ___ el (ow)   bl ___ ___ se (ou)   j ___ ful (oy)
c ___ n (oi)   j ___ elry (ew)   h ___ se (ou)

Encourage the children to select a diphthong on the chalkboard to complete each word. Direct the children to write each diphthong in the appropriate space and then to read the resulting word. You may want to challenge the children to create oral or written sentences using the resulting words.

To further develop the activity, you may wish to write the following words in a row at the top of the chalkboard: *stew, ground, point, down, boy.* Then write the following incomplete sentences.

1. *This pencil has a sharp _____ . (point)*
2. *Our family has two girls and one _____ . (boy)*
3. *She stood with her feet planted firmly on the _____ . (ground)*
4. *Drew likes to eat _____ for dinner. (stew)*
5. *The opposite of* up *is _____ . (down)*

Invite volunteers to select a word on the chalkboard to complete each sentence. Direct the children to write the word in the appropriate space and read aloud the completed sentence.

You may want to point out to the children that the *ow* in some words, such as *bow,* can have either a long vowel sound or the sound of a diphthong. Say the following sentences aloud, encouraging the children to identify the sound of the *ow* as a long vowel and the sound of *ow* as a diphthong.

1. *They will take a* bow *after the play is over.*
2. *She is wearing a pretty* bow.

74

Diphthongs

Say the name of the picture in each box. Circle the name.

1. toy / **boy** / ahoy / joy	2. drew / grew / **blew** / flew	3. **cloud** / clown / prowl / growl	4. now / row / own / **cow**
5. snout / snow / scowl / **scout**	6. owl / out / **oil** / oat	7. flew / drew / **screw** / crew	8. boys / **toys** / joys / ahoy
9. shower / sawed / **sewer** / sound	10. **boil** / foil / bout / pout	11. rouse / **mouse** / mound / found	12. towed / bowed / **towel** / trowel
13. soils / **coins** / rains / coils	14. rivalry / **jewelry** / joyful / jointly	15. cloud / loud / **clown** / crown	16. newsreel / **newspaper** / newer / sewer
17. blower / flower / slower / **shower**	18. **mountain** / county / **fountain** / bounty	19. **screwdriver** / chew / **driven** / show	20. avoiding / appoint / **noisemakers** / voice

NAME _____

Diphthongs **75**

Find the word in each box to complete the sentence. Circle the word. Then write it on the line.

1. A crowd saw the __royal__ family board the plane. | loyal / **royal** / yeast
2. We must learn how to avoid **poison** ivy in the woods. | person / **poison** / prison
3. Will your mother allow you to **join** the scouts? | gain / pain / **join**
4. The new ship and its **crew** are days overdue. | **crew** / screw / flew

Read the words that are part of each sentence. Finish the sentence by writing the words from the box in the correct order.

1. The girls tossed the _____ __coins in the fountain__ | in / the / fountain / coins
2. If you have your choice, will you go to __the beach or downtown__ | beach / the / downtown / or
3. Paul was the first boy at bat because he __drew the longest straw__ | the / straw / longest / drew
4. The wind blew out the camper's lantern as __the storm grew worse__ | worse / storm / the / grew
5. The teacher will appoint a boy or girl to report on the __noise in the hall__ | in / noise / hall / the
6. A crowd soon gathered on the street to enjoy the filming __of a TV show__ | show / a / TV / of

NAME _____

55

Beat-the-Card Game   Prepare a stack of word cards using words containing diphthongs, such as the following: *blouse, brown, crowd, flour, ground, joint, joyful, chew, poison, royal, grew, few, sound.*

Invite the children to sit or stand in front of you. Flash the first word card in front of the children and ask a child to spell the diphthong sound heard. If the child responds correctly, give the word card to the child. If the child responds incorrectly, keep the word card. Continue in the same manner until each child has had a turn.

Reteaching

Speaking   Display the following pictures or picture flashcards at the front of the classroom: *book, coins, jewelry, cloud, mow, pool, coat, mouse, steam, eight, towel.* Encourage the child to identify each picture and to write the name for it on the chalkboard. Then challenge the child to circle the words containing diphthongs and to use them in sentences. If the child identifies words incorrectly, provide encouragement by acknowledging the similarities between words with diphthongs and words with long vowel sounds.

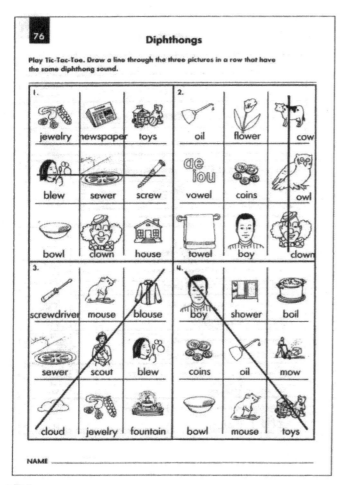

Lesson 34
Consonant Digraphs *CH* and *CK* (page 77)

Objective The child will distinguish between the sounds of the digraphs *ch* and *ck* and will read words containing these digraphs.

A consonant digraph consists of two consonants that together represent a new sound.

Review

Speaking To review the digraphs *th*, *wh*, *sh*, and *ch*, you may wish to display the following word cards at the front of the classroom: *thank, with, whale, wheat, shell, fish, cheap, when, leech, each.* Encourage volunteers to read each word aloud, to identify the consonant digraph, and to use the word in a sentence. Invite the children to explain in their own words the definition of a consonant digraph.

Teaching Ideas

Listening Write the following words in three columns on the chalkboard and ask volunteers to circle the consonant digraph or digraphs in each word as you say it aloud.

choice	school	Jack
chew	chorus	pick
church	echo	truck

Encourage the children to repeat each word in the first column and to identify the sound of the *ch* digraph. Repeat the activity with the second column. Then ask the children to identify the sound of *ck* in each of the words in the third column. Point out that the *ch* in school and the *ck* in Jack both have the sound of the letter *K*. Explain that *ch* appears at the beginning or the end of a word, but that *ck* comes only at the end of a word or a syllable.

Dueling-Digraphs Game Challenge the children with the Dueling-Digraphs Game. Display the following word cards at the front of the classroom: *pick, socket, back, porch, church, cricket.* Encourage a volunteer to choose a card to use in a digraph duel. Invite the volunteer to read the word aloud and to name another word containing the same digraph. Suggest that the volunteer choose a challenger to name a third word with the same digraph. If the challenger is correct, ask the volunteer to suggest a fourth word. Continue the round until one child gives an incorrect answer. Encourage the winner to choose another word card and begin a second round of play with a new challenger. Continue the game until all the word cards have been used.

Consonant Digraphs: CH, CK 77

Read each word below. Write the word in the first column if it has the sound *ch* has in cheese. Write the word in the second column if it has the sound *ch* and *ck* have in school and socks.

jacks	racket	chimney	children	teacher
echo	cheap	church	schedule	scheme
choice	nickel	chimpanzee	chocolate	character
kitchen	ranch	witch	pinch	chipmunk
chorus	cricket	picket	school	socket
chance		truck		ache

choice	jacks
chimney	racket
children	echo
teacher	schedule
cheap	character
church	scheme
chocolate	nickel
chipmunk	chorus
chimpanzee	cricket
kitchen	picket
ranch	school
witch	socket
pinch	ache
chance	truck

NAME _____

Lesson 35
Consonant Digraphs KN, GN, WR, and PH (pages 78–80)

Objective The child will associate the digraphs *kn*, *gn*, *wr*, and *ph* with the sounds they represent and will read words containing these digraphs.

Review

Reading To review the *ch* and *ck* consonant digraphs, you may wish to write the following sentences on the chalkboard.

1. *My arms ache from digging the ditch.*
2. *When the teacher left, the children made a racket.*
3. *Did Mitch get a chance to drive the tank truck?*

Then ask the children to read each sentence aloud and to circle the *ch* and *ck* words.

Teaching Ideas

Listening Write the following words in four columns on the chalkboard, and ask volunteers to circle the first two consonants in each word.

knife	*gnaw*	*wreck*	*photo*
knot	*gnarl*	*wrote*	*phonics*
knee	*gnash*	*wrist*	*Phillip*
knock	*gnome*	*wrong*	*Phyllis*

Encourage the children to read each word in the first column and to identify the beginning sound they hear in each word. Point out that the initial letter, *K*, is silent and the sound of the second letter, *N*, is heard. Repeat the procedure with the *gn* words in the second column and the *wr* words in the third column. Explain that *kn*, *gn*, and *wr* are called consonant digraphs. The letters *kn* and *gn* usually sound like the letter *N*. The letters *wr* usually sound like the letter *R*. Now continue with the words in the fourth column, pointing out that *ph* usually makes the sound of the letter *F*.

Surprise-Box Game Try challenging the children with the Surprise-Box Game. Write the words from the previous activity on small word cards and place them in a box. Divide the children into two teams and invite a player from each team to watch as you draw a word card at random. Let the child who is first to name the word and use it in a sentence earn a team point. Continue until all the word cards have been drawn.

Reading Write the following word groups on the chalkboard and encourage the children to read each group of words aloud.

gn: gnaw, gnash, no, gnu
wr: wreath, wing, wriggle, wreck
ph: phrase, pheasant, Phyllis, peasant
kn: kitchen, knock, knit, knew

Invite volunteers to tell which word in each group does not belong. Then challenge the children to explain why the words do not belong with the other three in each group.

Speaking For reinforcement, you may wish to write the following sentences on the chalkboard.

1. *Phyllis took the wreath into the living room.*
2. *Someone unknown to us won the contest.*
3. *Ralph read about a kind of antelope called a gnu.*
4. *I like a lot of knickknacks on the shelf.*

Encourage the children to read each sentence aloud and to identify the words containing *kn, gn, wr,* or *ph* digraphs.

Extension

Writing Write the following words on the chalkboard: *knack, photo, gnat, knit, wrestle, knee, gnaw, sign, typhoon.* Direct the child to write a sentence using each of the words on a separate sheet of paper. Then ask the child to copy the sentences, leaving blank spaces in place of the words with *kn, ph, gn,* or *wr* digraphs. Suggest that the child fill in the digraph for each of the words, leaving the rest of the word blank. You might encourage the child to ask a parent or another child to complete the unfinished words to solve the challenge sentences.

---

80   **Consonant Digraphs**

Find the word in each box to complete the sentence. Circle the word. Then write it on the line.

1. Do not forget to pack a frying pan in your _____ knapsack _____	knothole / knowledge / (knapsack)
2. Did you hear the echo when Phillip **shouted** , "Hello"?	stamped / (shouted) / cheered
3. Who knows the difference between a **typhoon** and a tornado?	typhoid / (typhoon) / typical
4. The main character in the story is a **charming** chimp.	scheme / changer / (charming)
5. Each of us has heard a symphony **orchestra** play.	(orchestra) / elephant / paragraph

Read the words that are part of each sentence. Finish the sentence by writing the words from the box in the correct order.

1. Ralph and _____ Chuck like to wrestle _____	like / Chuck / wrestle / to
2. A large African antelope is **known as a gnu**	known / gnu / as / a
3. Phyllis sent us a **good photo of herself**	herself / of / photo / good
4. Charles found parts of a wrecked **ship on the beach**	the / beach / on / ship
5. The man passed out free tickets **to the dolphin show**	dolphin / the / show / to

NAME _____

Lesson 36
Ending *LE* (pages 81–82)

Objective   The child will identify the sound of the ending *le* and will read words ending in *le*.

Review

Speaking   Write the following headings on the chalkboard: *beginning consonant, short vowel, long vowel, silent vowel, vowel digraph, consonant digraph, diphthong.* Then pronounce each of the following words and write them on the chalkboard: *typhoon, wreath, choice, knickknack, gnash, which, book, orchestra.* Point to the parts of each word and ask the children to identify each word part by selecting the correct heading.

Teaching Ideas

Listening   Write the following words on the chalkboard.

middle	*bubble*	*circle*
table	*people*	*needle*
syllable	*rectangle*	*pickle*
whistle	*kettle*	*turtle*
buckle	*needle*	*doodle*
marble	*people*	*able*

Explain to the children that the suffix *le* has the sound of the letter *L*. Point out that the final *e* is silent.

Encourage the children to circle the letters that make the final sound in each word.

Reading   Write the following sentences on the chalkboard or duplicate them on paper for the children.

1. *Please don't scribble on the table.*
2. *Would you like to eat a pickle or an apple?*
3. *Did you cut out a triangle or a rectangle?*
4. *Each of the people held a candle.*
5. *The eagle made a circle in the sky.*

Encourage volunteers to read the sentences aloud and to identify words that end in *le*.

To vary the activity, you might emphasize listening skills by reading the sentences aloud rather than writing them on the chalkboard or duplicating them. Challenge the children to identify the words in each sentence that end in *le*.

Extension

Art   Encourage the child to choose three words that end in *le* and to write them on a piece of paper. Suggest that the child imagine a scene that includes the three words and illustrate that scene.

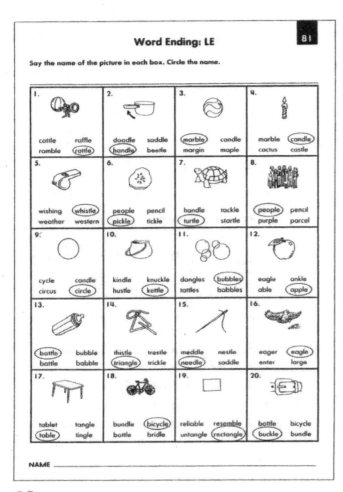

60

Unit 12 Syllables; Suffixes

Lesson 37
Vowels Seen and Heard (pages 83–84)

Objective The child will identify vowel sounds seen and heard in words with more than one syllable.

Review

Speaking To review the vowel rules learned in Units Three and Four, you may wish to write each of the following rules on the chalkboard: *Short Vowel Rule, Long Vowel Rule 1, Long Vowel Rule 2*. Encourage the children to read each rule aloud or to explain what each rule means. Invite volunteers to name words that follow each rule. You might want to write the children's words next to the appropriate rule.

Teaching Ideas

Listening Write the following vowel combinations as headings on the chalkboard: *ar, or, ir, ur, er, oo, ea, au, aw, ei, ow, ou, oi, oy, ew*. Then write words, such as the following, on the chalkboard as examples of words containing vowel combinations.

carpet	*raccoon*	*tower*	*loaner*	*breathy*
cloudy	*thirsty*	*faucet*	*burning*	*boiling*
lawsuit	*joyful*	*turning*	*eighteen*	*fewest*

Encourage the children to pronounce each word and rewrite it under the appropriate heading. Challenge the children to tell how many vowel sounds are heard in each word.

If you wish to extend the activity, invite volunteers to offer additional two-syllable words for each heading.

Seen-and-Heard Game Divide the class into two teams. Assign one team to tell how many vowels are heard in the words you will say. Assign the other team to tell how many vowels are seen in each word. Encourage the teams to work cooperatively to describe as many words as possible in a given time period. You may want to write each word on the chalkboard as you say it. If you wish, use the following words: *mop, football, scout, balloon, chain, lawn, carrot, join*.

Reteaching

Writing Write the following words in a column on the chalkboard or duplicate them in a column on paper: *bookworm, schoolroom, mermaid, yawn*. Encourage the child to write after each word the number of vowel sounds heard in the word and the number of vowels seen in the word.

To expand the activity, you might invite the child to write additional words in a column and to ask a partner to count the vowels seen and heard.

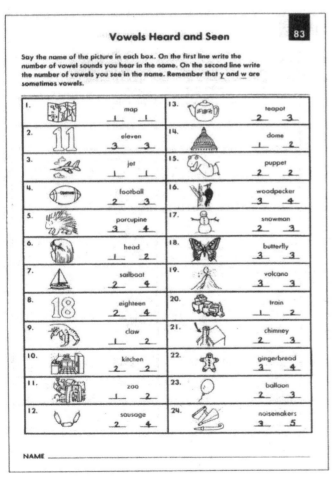

Lesson 38
Recognition of Syllables (pages 85–88)

Objective The child will recognize the syllables in words containing more than one syllable.

A syllable is a letter or group of letters in which one vowel sound is heard.

Review

Listening To reinforce the children's ability to listen to vowel sounds in words, you may wish to have the children tell how many vowel sounds are heard in each of the following words: *tornado, murmur, paper, farmer, reindeer, eight, football*. Invite volunteers, in turn, to distinguish between the number of vowels seen in each word after it is written and the number of vowel sounds heard in each word after it is spoken.

Teaching Ideas

Listening Say the word *puppy* aloud and encourage the children to repeat it after you. Then repeat the word while tapping out the syllables with your finger. Invite the children to do the same. Ask the children how many times they tapped. Point out that each tap accompanied one part, or syllable, of

the word *puppy*. Explain that words contain one syllable for each vowel sound heard. Write *puppy* on the chalkboard and have a volunteer identify the two vowel sounds in the word.

Next, say the following words aloud or present the following word cards for volunteers to read aloud: *cabin, grapes, rabbit, toys, iceberg, window, playground, mule, strawberry*. Encourage the children to tap out the syllables with their fingers as they say each word aloud.

Syllable-Riddle Game You may wish to challenge the children with the Syllable-Riddle Game. Write the following pairs of words on the chalkboard: *cherry/strawberry, window/door, kitten/dog, soup/sandwich*. Direct the children to refer to the word pairs as they answer the following riddles.

1. *It is a two-syllable word for a summer fruit. (cherry)*
2. *It is a one-syllable word for something you open. (door)*
3. *It is a two-syllable word for a pet. (kitten)*
4. *It is a one-syllable word for a part of a meal. (soup)*

After the children have answered the riddles correctly, encourage volunteers to create their own riddles for these word pairs and to pose them to the other children. Acknowledge the children who create riddles and those who answer them.

Writing Write the following compound words on the chalkboard and ask a volunteer to read them aloud.

footstep	*rosebud*	*upstairs*	*iceberg*
highway	*cobwebs*	*sagebrush*	*airport*
fishbowl	*lightbulb*	*baseball*	*sailboat*

Encourage the children to draw a line between the two words that are combined to make each compound word. If you wish, direct the children to count the syllables in each word and to write the number next to the word.

Extension

Art You might encourage the child to illustrate one or more words from the following list of compound words: *football, necklace, screwdriver, strawberry, headline, fishbowl.* Then suggest that the child think of other compound words to illustrate. Direct the child to illustrate each half of the compound word and to place a plus sign between the two illustrations. Explain that the illustrations may be serious or silly. If you wish to have the child share these illustrations with other members of the class, ask the child to draw a blank underneath each drawing for each letter of the word the drawing illustrates. Have other children guess the word and fill in the blanks with the correct letters to spell the word.

Family Involvement Activity Duplicate the Family Letter on page 94 of this Teacher's Edition. Send it home with the children.

Recognition of Syllables [87]

To recognize a new word, you often look at and pronounce small parts, or syllables, within the word, listening to see if you can recognize them as words you have used or heard before. To do this you may need to divide a word into syllables. Here are two tips to help you divide words into syllables.

Tip 1: A one-syllable word is never divided. (pass)
Tip 2: Divide a compound word between the words that form the compound word. (bath/robe)

Divide the following words into syllables, drawing a slash between each syllable. Write the number 1 or 2 after each word to show which tip you used. Remember that you can tell the number of syllables in a word by counting the vowel sounds you hear.

pass	teapot	oatmeal	breakfast
tiptop	sandbox	plate	house
fishbowl	strand	toothbrush	flashlight
perch	tadpole	dustpan	noise
sailboat		brook	

pass	1	oat/meal	2
tip/top	2	plate	1
fish/bowl	2	tooth/brush	2
perch	1	dust/pan	2
sail/boat	2	brook	1
tea/pot	2	break/fast	2
sand/box	2	house	1
strand	1	flash/light	2
tad/pole	2	noise	1

NAME _____

Recognition of Syllables [88]

Divide the following words into syllables, drawing a slash between each syllable. Write the number of 1 or 2 after each word to show which tip you used.

airport	woodpile	playpen	peanut	headline
curve	join	sagebrush	stairway	football
handcuffs	peacock	bedroom	march	beehive
iceberg	raincoat	necklace	headache	popcorn
dream	spend	proud	leaves	found
airplane		jigsaw		showmanship

air/port	2	neck/lace	2
curve	1	proud	1
hand/cuffs	2	jig/saw	2
ice/berg	2	pea/nut	2
dream	1	stair/way	2
air/plane	2	march	1
wood/pile	2	head/ache	2
join	1	leaves	1
pea/cock	2	head/line	2
rain/coat	2	foot/ball	2
spend	1	bee/hive	2
play/pen	2	pop/corn	2
sage/brush	2	found	1
bed/room	2	show/man/ship	2

NAME _____

Lesson 39
Suffixes *S, ED,* and *ES*   (pages 89–90)

Objective   The child will add the suffixes *s, ed,* or *es* to form new words.

If a base word ends in *x, ss, sh, ch,* or *z,* the suffix *es* forms the plural of the word. The suffix *es* is a syllable.

When the suffix *ed* is added to a base word ending in *d* or *t,* the suffix is pronounced *ed.* The suffix is then a syllable.

Review

Listening   To reinforce the children's recognition of syllables, you might wish to say the following words one at a time, asking the children to raise their hands when they hear a one-syllable word: *happy, home, toothbrush, ask, paper, pen, bookcase, paste, juice, football.*

Teaching Ideas

Listening   Write the following headings and words in two columns on the chalkboard: *dream, play, drink; burn, sail, talk.* Invite the children to read the words in the first column. Add an *s* to each word, explaining that the new addition at the end of the word is called a suffix. Explain that the suffix *s*

makes a word plural. Encourage volunteers to read the plural words aloud. Repeat the procedure with the words in the second column, using the suffix *ed* instead of *s.* Explain that the suffix *ed* places an action in the past. Ask for volunteers to read the new words aloud.

Speaking   Display the following word cards on the chalkboard ledge, and ask the children to read each word, identify the suffix, and repeat the sound of the suffix: *chopped, curled, sails, cleaned, floats, crossed, mailed.*

Writing   You might want to write the following words in two columns on the chalkboard: *box, dress, brush, bench, fizz; plant, load, mend, rest.* Point out that if a base word ends in *x, ss, sh, ch,* or *z,* the suffix *es* is added to create a plural. Invite the children to add the suffix *es* to the words in the first column and *ed* to the words in the second column. Encourage volunteers to read the resulting words aloud.

89

Suffixes: S, ED

Underline the base word and circle the suffix in each of the following words. Remember that a base word is a word to which a prefix or suffix may be added to form a new word.

1. bugs	2. failed	3. burned	4. crossed	5. rays
6. fussed	7. tarred	8. worked	9. cheered	10. thinks
11. wished	12. asked	13. fixed	14. spends	15. mailed
16. played	17. leads	18. snows	19. hatched	20. dreamed
21. puffed	22. helped	23. rained	24. plows	25. parted

Find the word in the box to complete each sentence. Circle the word. Then write the word on the line.

1. Mary will ____lead____ the other scouts to a secret cave.	(lead) / leads
2. Will Bob be able to ____fix____ the wrecked car?	(fix) / fixed
3. Roger dreamed that he ____sailed____ away on a white cloud.	sail / (sailed)
4. We have ____asked____ our teacher to take us to the zoo.	ask / (asked)
5. Ellen's class took their lunch and hiked up to the ____rock____ at the top of the hill.	(rock) / rocked
6. When the eggs were ready to ____hatch____, we saw the chicks peck their way out of the shells.	(hatch) / hatched

NAME _____

90

Suffixes: ES, ED

If a base word ends in x, ss, sh, ch, or z, we usually add es, which is a syllable, to form the plural of the word. Underline the base word in the words below. Circle the suffix.

1. branches	2. fuzzes	3. beads	4. wishes	5. boxes
6. taxes	7. losses	8. patches	9. sixes	10. glasses
11. ashes	12. beaches	13. kisses	14. seals	15. dishes
16. buzzes	17. axes	18. brushes	19. bosses	20. weights
21. lunches	22. passes	23. schools	24. shaws	25. thrushes
26. eggs	27. chairs	28. foxes	29. witches	30. mixes
31. misses	32. castles	33. birds	34. fizzes	35. punches

When ed is added to a base word ending in d or t, the suffix is a syllable and is pronounced ed. Circle the word that will complete the sentence. Write it on the line.

1. The boys ____coasted____ down the hill on their bicycles.	cranked / roasted / (coasted)
2. An empty raft ____floated____ downstream with the current.	bloated / (floated) / planted
3. The hot sun ____melted____ the ice before we could skate.	(melted) / rusted / sorted
4. Tom ____needed____ a screw or a nail to hang up the sign.	mended / (needed) / rested
5. The helicopter ____landed____ on the roof of the post office.	darted / loaded / (landed)
6. The girls made a windmill for a school project, and the boys ____painted____ it.	painted / (painted) / printed

NAME _____

64

Lesson 40
Suffixes *S, ES, ED,* and *ING* (page 91)

Objective   The child will form and will read words ending in *s, es, ed,* and *ing.*

Review

Writing   To practice forming plurals, you might wish to write the following words on the chalkboard: *tugboat, hairbrush, cobweb, chipmunk, wrench, boss, chorus, wreath.* Ask the children to add *s* or *es* to each of the words. Invite volunteers to read each plural word aloud.

Teaching Ideas

Speaking   Write the following words on the chalkboard: *drinking, sleeping, dreaming, asking, playing, frying.* Encourage the children to underline the base word, circle the suffix, and then read each word aloud.

Listening   Write the following words and sentences on the chalkboard.

help—Help *me carry this box upstairs.*

helps—Mary helps *her father clean the house.*

helped—Tom helped *me walk the dog.*

helping—Don is helping *me do my homework.*

Point out to the children that each form of the word *help* on the chalkboard tells when the act of helping happened. Challenge the children to tell when each action takes place. (You may need to clarify the time being referenced: help—either now or sometime in the near future; helps—anytime; helped—yesterday, in the past; and helping—exact time, now.)

Ending Game   Stack the following word cards facedown at the front of the classroom: *iron, plant, pick, drain, ask, want, break.* Then write the following headings in a row at the top of the chalkboard: *s, ed, ing.* Divide the class into two teams and ask a child from the first team to choose a word card from the stack and to read it aloud. Invite a child from the second team to write the word with the proper suffix under each heading. You might want to allow the players to consult with team members before writing the forms of the word on the chalkboard. Award the teams one point for each correct form of a word. Continue the game until all the word cards have been used.

Extension

Writing   Write the following words on the chalkboard or on paper and encourage the child to write a sentence for each word: *rides, driving, talked, eats, boxes, melted, singing, branches.* You might suggest that the child underline each base word.

Suffixes: S, E, ED, ING | 91

Read the words that are part of each sentence. Finish the sentence by choosing the correct base word in the box and adding the correct suffix— s, es, ed, or ing—to it. Write the word on the line.

1. The fence along the road needs _____mending_____ | send / (mend) / dart

2. Scouting is good _training_ for boys and girls. | track / brain / (train)

3. Roberta trimmed the bushes and the _branches_ of the trees with some clippers. | thrush / beach / (branch)

4. Acting out a story is more fun than _telling_ the story. | (tell) / fill / bell

5. Kurt places his hand over his mouth when he _coughs_ | squint / (cough) / paint

6. Are we _going_ to have fair weather for tomorrow's picnic? | (go) / no / so

7. Bill _squinted_ because he was facing the sun, searching for his lost balloon. | spend / splint / (squint)

8. Stop! Do not run and jump into the swimming pool. It has just been _drained_ | dream / train / (drain)

9. The elephants are _leading_ the circus parade down Main Street. | lend / (lead) / deal

10. Pat enjoys _reading_ letters she has received since she became ill. | reach / (read) / seat

11. Did the gnu know that the lion was _stalking_ him? | truck / stand / (stalk)

NAME _____

Lesson 41
Suffixes ER, EST, FUL, and LESS (pages 92–93)

Objective The child will form and will read words ending in the suffixes *er*, *est*, *ful*, and *less*.

Review

Speaking To practice identifying the sounds of the suffix *ed*, you may wish to display the following word cards and ask the children to read them aloud: *camped, burned, curled, darted, crossed, mailed, melted, sorted, poked, ticked*. For each word card, encourage a child to write the word on the chalkboard, underline each base word, circle the suffix, and say the sound of the suffix *ed*.

Teaching Ideas

Listening Draw the following trees on the chalkboard, explaining that the first tree is tall, the second is taller, and the third is the tallest.

Write the words *tall*, *taller*, and *tallest* under the appropriate trees. Explain that when two things are compared, the suffix *er* is used; when three things are compared, the suffix *est* is used. Encourage volunteers to use the words *taller* and *tallest* in sentences.

Speaking Write the following phrases on the chalkboard and ask the children to explain the meaning of each: *a restful sleep, a thankful boy, a careless girl, a useful job*. Write each suffix and its definition on the chalkboard, explaining that the suffix *ful* means *full of* and the suffix *less* means *without*. Encourage the children to use each phrase in a sentence.

Reteaching

Speaking Display each of the following word cards: *spotless, helpful, slower, worthless, strongest, playful, careful*. Challenge the child to read the word on the card, identify the base word and the suffix, and use the word in a sentence.

To vary the activity, you may wish to say each word aloud to the child. Ask the child to write the word on a piece of paper and to circle the suffix. Encourage the child to write a sentence using the word.

---

92   **Suffixes: ER, EST**

Underline each base word below. Circle each suffix.

1. faster / fastest	2. slower / slowest	3. darker / darkest	4. longer / longest	5. shorter / shortest
6. thicker / thickest	7. hardest / harder	8. stiffest / stiffer	9. softest / softer	10. nearer / nearest
11. quickest / quicker	12. loudest / louder	13. lower / lowest	14. greenest / greener	15. newest / newer

Read the words that are part of each sentence. Finish the sentence by adding **er** or **est** to the base word in the box. Write the new word on the line.

1. Which animal is ____slower____, a snail or a turtle?	slow
2. The __nearest__ store is five miles down the road.	near
3. At one time, clipper ships were the __fastest__ ships on the seas.	fast
4. To the little lambs, the grass looked __greener__ in the meadow across the road than in their meadow.	green
5. A rectangle is __longer__ than it is wide.	long
6. Our new sofa is __softer__ than the old one.	soft
7. My new shortcut is the __quickest__ way to school.	quick
8. The new owners of the castle made the __darkest__ room into the lightest room by adding windows.	dark

NAME _____

---

93   **Suffixes: FUL, LESS**

Underline each base word below. Circle each suffix.

1. fearful / fearless	2. hopeless / hopeful	3. careless / careful	4. painful / painless	5. fearful / fearless
6. helpless / helpful	7. tactful / tactless	8. faithful / faithless	9. useless / useful	10. needless / needful
11. tasteful / tasteless	12. thankful / thankless	13. harmful / harmless	14. restless / restful	15. cheerless / cheerful

Read each sentence. Circle the word in the box that describes what the sentence is saying.

1. Some children cry when the barber cuts their hair.	(tearful) / tearless
2. The mining engineers gave up the search for the lost mine.	hopeful / (hopeless)
3. Mr. Smith saw the puppy floating on a raft in the flooded stream, and he saved it.	(helpful) / helpless
4. We always lock all the windows and doors before we leave the house to go shopping.	(careful) / careless
5. The children huddled in the corner of the dark, chilly room.	cheerful / (cheerless)
6. Jill's hamburger had little flavor without salt and pepper.	tasteful / (tasteless)
7. Kitty clung to her big sister's hand as they ran down the dark street.	(fearful) / fearless
8. Rat and insect poisons must be kept out of children's reach.	(harmful) / harmless

NAME _____

66

Lesson 42
Suffixes *LY* and *NESS*   (page 94)

Objective   The child will form and will read words containing the suffixes *ly* and *ness*.

Review

Listening   To practice recognition of syllables, you might wish to say the following words one at a time, directing the children to tell how many syllables are heard in each: *showmanship, melted, training, lightest, wanted, cheers, cheerfulness.* You might have the children tap each syllable while saying each word.

Teaching Ideas

Listening   Write the following words on the chalkboard, asking the children to read each word aloud and to identify the suffix in each: *sadly, loudness, neatly, slowly, softness, quietly.* (Keep the *ly* words on the chalkboard for the following activity.)

Speaking   Explain to the children that the suffix *ly* answers the question *how* something is done. Encourage the children to use the words on the chalkboard to answer the following questions that you will ask.

1. How did Sandra whisper the secret?
2. How did the turtle move?
3. How did Cary arrange the pencils?

You might wish to have those children who respond correctly pose questions that have as answers the remaining words.

Writing   As further development, you might write the following words in a column on the chalkboard: *quick, loud, neat, soft.* Invite volunteers to add the suffix *ly* or the suffix *ness* to each word and to write a sentence using the new word on the chalkboard.

Extension

Writing   Duplicate the following words and incomplete sentences on paper or write them on the chalkboard: *thickly, gladly, neatly, quickly, thickness, gladness, neatness, quickness.*
1. The _____ of the book was three inches.
2. Manuel goes to swimming practice _____ .
3. Hamil's _____ makes his work easy to read.
4. Sue will complete these exercises _____ .

Encourage the child to read each sentence and to supply the appropriate word in the correct form. Suggest that the child circle the suffix of each word used. You might have the child use each of the unused words in written sentences.

---

94   Suffixes: LY, NESS

Underline each base word below. Circle each suffix.

1. largely / largeness	2. likely / likeness	3. dryness / dryly	4. crossness / crossly	5. closely / closeness
6. shortly / shortness	7. hardness / hardly	8. stiffly / stiffness	9. fairly / fairness	10. gladness / gladly
11. strangeness / strangely	12. thickness / thickly	13. weakly / weakness	14. neatly / neatness	15. quickness / quickly

Read the words that are part of each sentence. Finish the sentence by adding *ly* or *ness* to the base word in the box. Write the new word on the line.

1. The __likeness__ between Dick and his father is amazing.	like
2. Our __weekly__ newspaper had a report about our play.	week
3. The fire chief __proudly__ pinned badges for bravery on three members of our class.	proud
4. A diamond can scratch glass because of its __hardness__	hard
5. Please pass the ball __quickly__ around the circle.	quick
6. The dog's __tameness__ made it a nice pet for the children.	tame
7. The whiteness of the marble statue contrasts with the __blackness__ of the velvet drape behind it.	black
8. The grocery store worker stacked the canned goods __neatly__	neat

NAME _____

67

Lesson 43
Suffixes *EN* and *ABLE* (page 95)

Objective   The child will form and read words ending in the suffixes *en* and *able*.

Teaching Ideas

Writing   Write the following words in two columns on the chalkboard: *enjoyable, wearable, workable, cleanable; strengthen, blacken, lighten, soften.* Ask the children to read the words in the first column and to circle the suffix. Explain that the suffix *able* is added to a word to make it mean *is able to do something.* Repeat the procedure with the words in the second column, explaining that the suffix *en* means *to become* or *to have something.* Encourage the children to give the meaning of each word on the chalkboard. (You might write each of these suffixes on the chalkboard as a reference.)

Speaking   Write the following words on the chalkboard: *washable, sharpen, shorten, readable, thicken, movable, weaken, breakable.* Encourage the children to refer to these words to answer riddles you will pose.

1. *When a skirt is too long and needs a hem, what can be done to it?*
2. *Glass shatters because it has this quality.*
3. *If you can clean it in the washing machine, what is it?*
4. *When you give a pencil a point, what do you do to it?*

To continue this activity, encourage volunteers to create their own riddles for the rest of the words on the chalkboard.

Extension

Writing   Write the following incomplete sentences and base words on the chalkboard.

1. *The pudding will _____ as it cools. (thick)*
2. *Please _____ my pencil. (sharp)*
3. *Is this sweater _____? (wash)*
4. *Please _____ your seat belt. (fast)*
5. *I found this story very _____. (read)*
6. *This banana will _____ the cereal. (sweet)*

Direct the child to add *en* or *able* to each base word, and then to use the word to complete the sentence. If you wish, encourage the child to read the completed sentences to you.

Suffixes: EN, ABLE   95

Underline each base word below. Circle each suffix.

1. hard(en)	2. enjoy(able)	3. read(able)	4. black(en)	5. clean(able)
6. kiss(able)	7. sick(en)	8. weak(en)	9. wear(able)	10. reason(able)
11. strength(en)	12. thick(en)	13. short(en)	14. sweet(en)	15. beat(able)
16. train(able)	17. work(able)	18. fresh(en)	19. moist(en)	20. drink(able)
21. maid(en)	22. sharp(en)	23. dark(en)	24. quick(en)	25. laugh(able)

Read the words that are part of each sentence. Finish the sentence by adding **en** or **able** to the base word in the box. Write the new word on the line.

1. Daily exercises will __strengthen__ the muscles.	strength
2. My grandmother's shaky handwriting is not __readable__	read
3. The day we spent at the carnival was most __enjoyable__	enjoy
4. This lemonade is too sour. Please __sweeten__ it for us.	sweet
5. The water at camp is so bad that it is hardly __drinkable__	drink
6. There is so much paint on these pants that they are not __wearable__	wear
7. You may __sharpen__ your pencils the first thing each morning.	sharp
8. If you __moisten__ your finger and hold it in the air, you can tell which way the wind is blowing.	moist

NAME _____

68

Lesson 44
Suffixes *TION* and *SION* (page 96)

Objective The child will form and read words with the suffixes *tion* and *sion*.

Teaching Ideas

Listening Write the following words in two columns on the chalkboard: *action, vacation, motion, invitation, collection; confusion, division, invasion, occasion*. Ask the children to identify the sound of the ending syllable as you say each word aloud.

Speaking Display the following word cards on the chalkboard ledge: *station, vision, nation, motion, conclusion, election, addition*. Then say each of the following sentences.

1. The train stops at the _____ .
2. Another word for country is _____ .
3. When something moves, it is in _____ .
4. A person's eyesight is called _____ .
5. When you use a plus sign, you are doing _____ .
6. We vote for leaders in an _____ .
7. The end of a story is the _____ .

Encourage the children to choose a word from the word cards to complete each of the sentences. If you wish, ask the children to write the words on the chalkboard and to circle the suffix in each.

Reteaching

Listening Pronounce each of the following words: *conclusion, election, decision, notion, donation, vision, conversion, exception*. Ask the child to tell whether the word ends in *tion* or *sion*.

To extend the activity, ask the child to spell each word or to write it on the chalkboard.

Extension

Speaking Write the following words on small word cards and place them in a box: *confusion, division, vacation, multiplication, satisfaction, occasion, invasion*. Direct the child to select a word card from the box. Have the child read the word and then circle the suffix. Challenge the child to use the word in a sentence.

96

Suffixes: TION, SION

The endings tion and sion stand for sounds like shun or zhun. Read the words below. Underline each tion ending. Circle each sion ending.

1. action	2. vacation	3. division	4. motion	5. donation
6. addition	7. confusion	8. invitation	9. occasion	10. mention
11. nation	12. multiplication	13. collection	14. election	15. exception
16. pension	17. education	18. invasion	19. conclusion	20. excursion
21. notion	22. convention	23. satisfaction	24. introduction	25. subtraction

Find the word in each box to complete the sentence. Circle the word. Then write it on the line.

1. A wedding is a happy __occasion__	mention / **occasion** / donation
2. Carla sent each classmate an **invitation** to her party.	convention / collection / **invitation**
3. The **motion** of the subway made it hard to stand.	**motion** / notion / nation
4. Noise in a classroom causes **confusion** for all of us.	excursion / conclusion / **confusion**
5. Our family took an **excursion** boat up the river last Sunday.	**excursion** / conclusion / confusion
6. Matt invited Todd to visit during the spring **vacation**	addition / **vacation** / donation
7. Quick **action** saved the a boy who fell into the river.	notion / **action** / notion
8. Think about the story and write your own **conclusion**	convention / connection / **conclusion**

NAME _____

69

Lesson 45
Recognition of Syllables (pages 97–98)

Objective The child will apply Syllabication Tips 1 through 3 to divide words into syllables.

Syllabication Tip 1: A one-syllable word is never divided. (*pass*)

Syllabication Tip 2: Divide a compound word between the words that form the compound word. (*bath/robe*)

Syllabication Tip 3: When a word has a suffix, divide the word between the base word and the suffix if the suffix has a vowel sound. (*fear/less*)

Review

Listening To give children practice in auditory recognition of syllables, say the following words and ask the children to tap out the syllables in each: *useful, needed, grapes, greenest, hopeful, newer, section, thicken, mission, strangely.* You may need to remind the children that a word has one syllable for each vowel sound that can be heard.

Teaching Ideas

Writing Write each of the syllabication tips on the chalkboard, and ask the children to read them aloud. Then write the following words in three columns: *tag, pet, dog; toothbrush, bathroom, footprint; eating, rusty, harden.* Encourage the children to write next to each word the number of syllables heard in that word and then to circle the words that can be divided into syllables.

To expand the activity, ask the children to write each word and insert a slash between syllables. (You will want to keep the Syllabication Tips on the chalkboard for several lessons.)

Extension

Writing Prepare a worksheet with the following words: *pan, dreaming, roasted, closely, airport.* Have the child indicate the syllable break in each word with a slash. Encourage the child to apply the Syllabication Tips 1 through 3 to justify each syllable break.

Recognition of Syllables — 97

Tip 1. A one-syllable word is never divided. (pass)
Tip 2. Divide a compound word between the words that form the compound word. (bath/robe)
Tip 3. When a word has a suffix, divide the word between the base word and the suffix if the suffix has a vowel sound. (fear/less)

Divide the words below into syllables, drawing a slash between each syllable. After each word write the number of the tip you used. Remember that you can tell the number of syllables in a word by counting the vowel sounds you hear.

tasteless	nation	freshen	playground
hitches	caused	quickly	neatness
cattails	telling	longest	louder
likely	faithful	pension	mended
stiff	painted	glasses	pinching

taste/less	3	fresh/en	3
hitch/es	3	quick/ly	3
cat/tails	2	long/est	3
like/ly	3	pen/sion	3
stiff	1	glass/es	3
na/tion	3	play/ground	2
caused	1	neat/ness	3
tell/ing	3	loud/er	3
faith/ful	3	mend/ed	3
paint/ed	3	pinch/ing	3

NAME _____

Recognition of Syllables — 98

Divide the words below into syllables by drawing a slash between the syllables, as in the example. After each word write the number of the tip you used.

1. use/ful 3	2. hair/cut 2	3. squint/ing 3	4. plant/ed 3
5. need/ed 3	6. glad/ly 3	7. help/less 3	8. dark/er 3
9. grapes 1	10. brush/es 3	11. ac/tion 3	12. weak/ly 3
13. cross/ness 3	14. fear/less 3	15. mis/sion 3	16. thank/ful 3
17. green/est 3	18. rained 1	19. dry/ness 3	20. strange/ly 3
21. new/er 3	22. sweet/en 3	23. rain/coat 2	24. mix/es 3
25. dream/ing 3	26. sec/tion 3	27. proud/est 3	28. weak/en 3
29. taste/less 3	30. hope/ful 3	31. sick/en 3	32. sea/coast 2

Read the words that are part of each sentence. Finish the sentence by writing the words from the box in the correct order.

1. The Smiths have the _greenest lawn in town_	town / in / lawn / greenest
2. It rained soon after we _finished planting the corn_	planting / corn / finished / the
3. Two flash floods this past year _have weakened the dam_	have / dam / the / weakened
4. Quick action by the second _baseman saved the game_	the / saved / baseman / game
5. Because of its skin thickness, an elephant _is not easily hurt_	is / easily / hurt / not
6. To fill the crate, we need three _more boxes of berries_	of / boxes / more / berries

NAME _____

Lesson 46
Prefixes *UN* and *DIS*   (page 99)

Objective   The child will form and read words containing the prefixes *un* and *dis*.

A prefix is a syllable placed before a base word to form a new word.

Review

Listening   To give children practice in dividing words into syllables, write the following words on the chalkboard and have the children divide them into syllables: *driveway, painless, bathrobe, dresses, teacher, disband, unsafe, hopeless*.

Teaching Ideas

Speaking   Tell the children the definition of *prefix*. Write the following words on the chalkboard and ask the children to circle the prefixes in each: *unkind, unsafe, unused; dislike, dishonest, dissatisfy*. Explain that the prefix *un* usually means *not* and the prefix *dis* usually means *does not* or *is not*.

(You might write these prefixes and their definitions on the chalkboard as a reference.) Ask the children to read the words on the chalkboard and to explain the meaning of each word.

Extension

Writing   Duplicate the following sentences and prefix meanings, or write them on the chalkboard.
1. *The gas bill is still _____ paid. (not)*
2. *He never _____ obeys my parents. (does not)*
3. *John is _____ certain about the way home. (not)*
4. *Jane is still _____ pleased with her rock collection. (is not)*
5. *I didn't mean to be _____ kind. (not)*

Direct the child to read the sentences, adding the correct prefix to each incomplete word. If you wish, encourage the child to read each completed sentence aloud.

Family Involvement Activity   Duplicate the Family Letter on page 95 of this Teacher's Edition. Send it home with the children.

Prefixes: UN, DIS   `99`

A prefix is a syllable placed before a base word to create a new word. A prefix always has a particular meaning.
The prefixes un and dis usually reverse the meaning of a base word, as in unhappy and disobey.

Underline the base word and circle the prefix in each of the words below.

1. disclose	2. unknown	3. displease	4. discolor	5. unhandy
6. unjust	7. disown	8. dislike	9. unscrew	10. disagree
11. disable	12. unpack	13. dishonest	14. uneven	15. unused
16. unhappy	17. dislocate	18. unclaimed	19. disorder	20. discharge
21. disband	22. unwilling	23. disappear	24. untaught	25. uncertain

Find the word in each box to complete the sentence. Circle the word. Then write it on the line.

1. The post office will auction off packages that are ___unclaimed___	unclean / uncommon / (unclaimed)
2. Paul enjoys eating string beans, but he ___dislikes___ spinach.	disposes / (dislikes) / discolor
3. The ___unhappy___ clown painted a happy expression on his face.	unloaded / (unhappy) / unlocked
4. The corner lot will not make a good tennis court because the ground is ___uneven___	(uneven) / unfair / unearth
5. The wise prospector did not ___disclose___ the location of the new gold mine.	discard / (disclose) / discharge
6. You will ___displease___ your classmates if you quit the swimming team.	disappear / (displease) / disagree

NAME _____

Lesson 47
Prefixes *DE* and *EX*   (page 100)

Objective   The child will form and read words containing prefixes *de* and *ex*.

Teaching Ideas

Speaking   Write the following words in two columns on the chalkboard, asking the children to read each word aloud: *depart, descend, defrost; exchange, exhale, explain*. Underline the prefix in each word as the children say the word aloud. Explain that *de* means *down from* or *away from*. Ask the children to use each word from the first column in a sentence. Then explain that *ex* means *from* or *out of,* and ask the children to use each word in the second column in a sentence. (You might write these prefixes and their definitions on the chalkboard as a reference.)

Write the following sentences on the chalkboard.

1. *The express bus departed from the station quickly.*
2. *Our team expected to defeat the Tigers at softball.*
3. *The elevator descended quickly to the basement.*
4. *Please describe the rock display at the library.*

Invite volunteers to read a sentence and to circle the words containing the prefixes *de* and *ex*. Encourage the children to name other words having the same prefixes.

Listening   Slowly read each of the following sentences to the children and ask them to identify the words with the prefixes *de* and *ex* in each sentence.

1. *Will you exchange your skateboard for this mitt?*
2. *We detrained at the 125th Street Station.*
3. *Please excuse me for being late.*
4. *It was not easy to decode the secret message.*

Write the words with prefixes on the chalkboard as the children identify them. Encourage the children to restate each sentence without using the prefix.

Extension

Writing   Write the following words on the chalkboard: *decrease, explode, excuse, depart, defeat, explain*. Challenge the child to write an adventure story using at least four of the words on the chalkboard. Encourage the child to illustrate the story with original drawings. If you wish, suggest that the child share the completed story with the other children in the class.

---

100   Prefixes: DE, EX

The prefix **de** usually means down from or away from or the opposite of, as in depress, depart, and defrost.
The prefix **ex** means out from or beyond, as in extract, export, and exile.

Circle the prefix in each of the words below.

1. exchange	2. depend	3. depart	4. exclaim	5. deform
6. defrost	7. exile	8. descend	9. depart	10. exhale
11. deface	12. depress	13. expand	14. explode	15. decode
16. extend	17. explain	18. define	19. defeat	20. extract
21. decrease	22. express	23. except	24. denote	25. describe
26. excuse	27. demand	28. denounce	29. demerit	30. excerpt

Find the word in each box to complete the sentence. Circle the word. Then write the word on the line.

1. When we breathe, we inhale and ___exhale___	excuse / exile / (exhale)
2. Dogs and other pets must __depend__ on their owners for food.	(depend) / depart / depart
3. We had to __defrost__ the car's windshield because it was covered with ice.	describe / (defrost) / depress
4. The balloon hit a sharp object and __exploded__	expressed / (exploded) / exclaimed
5. Bees __extract__ nectar from flowers and make it into honey.	(extract) / excuse / explain
6. In the play-off game, Jan's team hopes to __defeat__ June's team.	deform / define / (defeat)

NAME _____

72

Lesson 48
Prefixes *RE* and *MIS* (page 101)

Objective The child will form and read words containing prefixes *re* and *mis*.

Teaching Ideas

Speaking Write the following words in two columns on the chalkboard: *redecorate, rewrite, repay; misspell, misfortune, misprint*. Ask the children to read each word in the first column. Underline the prefix as the children say the words aloud. Repeat the procedure with the words in the second column. Explain to the children that *re* means *again* or *back* and *mis* means *bad* or *wrong*. (You might write these prefixes and their definitions on the chalkboard as a reference.) Then ask the following questions.

1. Which word means decorate again?
2. Which word means write again?
3. Which word means spell wrong?
4. Which word means print wrong?
5. Which word means pay back?
6. Which word means bad fortune?

Keep the words on the chalkboard for the following activity.

Writing Encourage the children to write sentences using words from the previous activity. Direct them to circle the prefixes *re* and *mis* whenever they appear in the sentences.

You might continue the activity by asking the children to rewrite their sentences on another sheet of paper, leaving blanks where the *re* and *mis* words should be. Encourage the children to trade papers with their classmates and to complete each other's sentences.

Reading Write the following sentences on the chalkboard, and ask the children to circle the correct word in each sentence and then to read the completed sentence aloud.

1. I must (rewrite, miswrite) my paper.
2. Marvin (misplaces, replaces) his library books.
3. He always (repronounces, mispronounces) my name.
4. I promise to (repay, mispay) the money I borrowed.

Reteaching

Writing Duplicate the following sentences, or write them on the chalkboard.

1. I always *spell* her name *wrong*.
2. We are *not happy* with the rainy weather.
3. My brother is *not satisfied* with his new car.
4. He never *pronounces* a word *wrong*.

Direct the child to read the sentences and to substitute words with prefixes for each set of underlined words.

73

Lesson 49
Prefixes A, AC, AD, and IN (page 102)

Objective   The child will form and read words containing the prefixes *a*, *ac*, *ad*, and *in*.

Review

Listening   To give children practice with dividing words into syllables, write the following words on the chalkboard and ask the children to tap out the syllables for each: *matchbox, planted, nearest, blackness, wrench, foxes, woodpile*. Encourage the children to write the words on their paper and to indicate the syllable break in each word with a hyphen. (You may want to display the Syllabication Tips from Lesson 45 for the children's reference.)

Teaching Ideas

Reading   Tell the children that the prefixes *a*, *ac*, and *ad* can mean *to*. Explain that the prefix *in* can mean *in* or *not*. Then write the following words on the chalkboard, and read them to the children: *asleep, aboard, acclaim, account, adapt, adjoin, indigestion, inland*. Invite volunteers to circle the prefix in each word. (You might write each prefix and its definition on the chalkboard as a reference.) Help the children discover the meanings of words with prefixes by providing context sentences. Invite volunteers, in turn, to read the following sentences and give the meaning of the underlined word in each.

1. The baby is *asleep*.
2. Let us go *aboard* the ship.
3. Jed got *indigestion* from too much cake.
4. The explorers traveled *inland*.
5. Can we go *ashore* yet?
6. Our land *adjoins* Grandfather's land.
7. The band *accompanies* the rock star.

Extension

Writing   Duplicate the following sentences, or write them on the chalkboard.

1. The two children are __ way at school.
2. Please __ clude me in your plans to go camping.
3. We moved to a different __ dress.
4. Tasha __ cused me of taking her favorite pencil.
5. That man hates to __ mit his mistakes.

Encourage the child to read the sentences and to add the correct prefix to the incomplete word in each. If you wish, encourage the child to read each completed sentence aloud.

---

102   Prefixes: A, AC, AD, IN,

The prefix **a** usually means *to, at,* or *in,* as in *asleep* and *aboard.*
The prefix **ad** means *to,* as in *adapt* and *adjoin.*
The prefix **ac** also means *to,* but is used before base words beginning with *c, k,* or *q,* as in *accustom, acknowledge,* and *acquit.*
The prefix **in** means *in* or *not,* as in *instep* and *incurable.*

Circle the prefix in each of the words below.

1. asleep	2. inflate	3. accept	4. aboard	5. inside
6. invent	7. adrift	8. admit	9. acclaim	10. alike
11. accuse	12. inhuman	13. apart	14. away	15. address
16. awhile	17. amass	18. invite	19. acquire	20. across
21. involve	22. account	23. agree	24. include	25. ablaze
26. avert	27. incurable	28. adjust	29. alight	30. indigestion

Find the word in each box to complete the sentence. Circle the word. Then write it on the line.

1. His little sister asked him to ____address____ the birthday card.	**address** / adjoin / adjust
2. Because of injuries, several of the team's players are __inactive__	instep / **inactive** / inflame
3. When a train is ready to leave a station, the conductor shouts, "All __aboard__ ."	agree / awhile / **aboard**
4. Will you include me in the list of people you __invite__ to your party?	**invite** / invent / involve
5. If you __accept__ the invitation, you must help to make the party a success.	access / **accept** / accent

NAME _____

74

Lesson 50
Recognition of Syllables (pages 103–104)

Objective The child will apply Syllabication Tips 1, 2, 3, and 4 to divide words into syllables.

Syllabication Tip 4: When a word has a prefix, divide the word between the prefix and the base word. (*un/fair*)

Review

Reading Write Syllabication Tips 1, 2, and 3 on the chalkboard, and invite a volunteer to read them aloud. Encourage the children to provide examples of how the tips apply to actual words. If you like, suggest the following words: *darken, glasses, stiff, bathroom, carport.* Encourage the children to use the tips to help them divide the words into syllables. You might want to remind the children that every syllable must contain one vowel sound.

Teaching Ideas

Writing Say each of the following words: *unfair, alike, acclaim, replant, mislead, depart, admire, disown, inflame, exhale.* Ask volunteers to write a word on the chalkboard and to circle the prefix in it. Point out to the children that each prefix has a vowel sound. Keep these words on the chalkboard for the following activity.

Add Syllabication Tip 4 to the list of tips on the chalkboard, and encourage the children to read it aloud. Ask volunteers to choose a word from the previous activity and rewrite the word on the chalkboard, placing a slash between the syllables. Note: In some cases, more than one syllabication tip may apply for word divisions. For example, *inland* may be described by children as a compound word or a word with a prefix. Therefore, you might want to deemphasize the number of the syllabication tips and concentrate on the principles behind each tip. (Keep the tips on the chalkboard for the next lesson.)

Extension

Writing Pronounce the following words for the child, and ask the child to write them on the chalkboard or a sheet of paper: *bathtub, useful, talking, misplace, airplane, harden, replant, defrost, hallway, neatness.* Encourage the child to draw a slash between the syllables of each word.

Recognition of Syllables — 103

Tip 1: A one-syllable word is never divided. (pass)
Tip 2: Divide a compound word between the words that form the compound word. (bathrobe)
Tip 3: When a word has a suffix, divide the word between the base word and the suffix if the suffix has a vowel sound. (fear/less)
Tip 4: When a word has a prefix, divide the word between the prefix and the base word. (un/fair)

Divide the words below into syllables, drawing a slash between each syllable. After each word, write the number of the tip you used. You may need to use more than one tip to divide some words.

invite	airplane	extending	rained
accepted	involve	admit	depress
dream	defroster	discharge	acquit
misplace	disclose	unfairly	unscrew
expanded	displaying	resharpen	misbehave

in/vite	4	ex/tend/ing	3,4
ac/cept/ed	3,4	ad/mit	4
dream	1	dis/charge	4
mis/place	4	un/fair/ly	3,4
ex/pand/ed	3,4	re/sharp/en	3,4
air/plane	2	rained	1
in/volve	4	de/press	4
de/frost/er	3,4	ac/quit	4
dis/close	4	un/screw	4
dis/play/ing	3,4	mis/be/have	4

NAME _____

Recognition of Syllables — 104

Divide the words below into syllables by drawing a slash between the syllables, as in the example. Some words may have one syllable.

1. a/board	2. ac/cept	3. ex/cept	4. a/bide
5. un/like/ly	6. de/fine	7. dis/cuss	8. ex/press
9. streets	10. ad/mit	11. fore/cast/ing	12. wake/ful
13. in/quire	14. un/dress	15. burned	16. un/real
17. dis/grace	18. de/cid/ed/ly	19. a/while	20. mis/take
21. kind/ness	22. hand/springs	23. re/phrase	24. ex/port/ed
25. re/mois/ten	26. de/fens/less	27. dis/trus/ful	28. mis/print/ing
29. re/peat/ed/ly	30. un/shav/en	31. sea/side	32. dis/joint/ed

Read the words that are part of each sentence. Finish the sentence by writing the words from the box in the correct order.

1. Please accept this gift as an _____expression of my thanks	of my expression thanks
2. After school there will be a contest to decide the gymnastics champion	gymnastics decide the champion
3. Think beforehand what you will need to take on your trip	take trip your on
4. Perhaps I can answer your question if you rephrase it	it you if rephrase
5. Mom has repeatedly told us to take off our muddy shoes at the door	the door at shoes
6. All of the Jones family are going to the beach except the father, who has to work	has work to who

NAME _____

Unit 14 Syllabication

Lesson 51
Recognition of Syllables (pages 105–107)

Objective The child will apply Syllabication Tips 1 through 5 to divide words into syllables.

Syllabication Tip 5: When two or more consonants come between two vowels in a word, the word is usually divided between the consonants. (*bet/ter*) Be careful not to split blends or digraphs.

Review

Reading To give children practice with dividing words containing prefixes, write the following words on the board and ask the children to underline the prefix in each: *infield, adrift, invest, asleep, adjoin.* Encourage volunteers to each draw a slash to divide a word into syllables. Encourage the children to explain the syllabication tip that applies to words with prefixes.

Teaching Ideas

Reading Add Syllabication Tip 5 to those tips already on the chalkboard and ask a volunteer to read it aloud. Then write the following words on the chalkboard: *pencil, picture, basket, pillow, lesson, rabbit, tunnel, candy, purple.* Ask a volunteer to read the first word aloud and to answer the following questions.

1. *How many vowels do you see in* pencil?
2. *How many vowels do you hear?*
3. *How many consonants separate the two vowels?*
4. *According to Syllabication Tip 5, where should the word be divided?*

After the volunteer has answered the questions correctly, rewrite the word with a slash designating the syllable break. Repeat the procedure with each of the other words on the chalkboard. Keep the five tips on the chalkboard for the next lesson.

Speaking Ask a volunteer to read each of the five syllabication tips on the chalkboard. Then write the following words on the chalkboard: *untie, hornet, rainbow, toe, handed, sandwiches, repaint, garden, mailed, popcorn.* Encourage volunteers to read each word, identify the syllabication tip that applies, and then draw a slash mark to designate the break in syllables.

Write the following sentences on the chalkboard.

1. *Max plans to repaint his summer home.*
2. *I cannot dry the dishes for you.*
3. *We put the broken fishbowl into the trash can.*
4. *Tim refused to eat his supper.*

Recognition of Syllables — page 105

Tip 5: When two or more consonants come between two vowels, the word is usually divided between the first two consonants. (bet/ter) Do not split blends or digraphs.

Divide the words below into syllables by drawing a slash between the syllables.

1. com/plete	2. pen/cil	3. con/fess	4. sud/den
5. tor/ment	6. neck/lace	7. prac/tice	8. tar/get
9. pur/ple	10. chil/dren	11. sur/prise	12. con/tents
13. shal/low	14. dic/tate	15. pic/ture	16. pret/zel
17. hand/y	18. rub/bers	19. kitch/en	20. post/man

Read the words that are part of each sentence. Finish the sentence by writing the words from the box in the correct order.

1. The police perform an important _service for our community_	service our for community
2. Christine and Colleen like to _play basketball after school_	basketball after play school
3. Jan's pretty purple balloon got caught in the _branches of a tree_	tree branches a of
4. Children like to wade _in the shallow water_	in shallow the water
5. Theresa went to the kitchen _and ate some pretzels_	ate some and pretzels
6. The visit from the prince was a _surprise to the princess_	to princess the surprise

NAME _____

Recognition of Syllables — page 106

Tip 1: A one-syllable word is never divided. (pass)
Tip 2: Divide a compound word between the words that form the compound word. (bathrobe)
Tip 3: When a word has a suffix, divide the word between the base word and the suffix if the suffix has a vowel sound. (fear/less)
Tip 4: When a word has a prefix, divide the word between the prefix and the base word. (un/fair)
Tip 5: When two or more consonants come between two vowels in a word, the word is usually divided between the first two consonants. (bet/ter) Do not split blends or digraphs.

Divide the words below into syllables, drawing a slash between each syllable. After each word write the number or numbers of the tips you used.

knife	surfboard	foxes	matchbox
restless	blackness	slower	depart
discarded	quickly	nearest	wrench
downspout	respectfully	extension	reception

knife	1	fox/es	3
rest/less	3	slow/er	3
dis/card/ed	3,4	near/est	3
down/spout	2	ex/ten/sion	3,4
surf/board	2	match/box	2
black/ness	3	de/part	4
quick/ly	3	wrench	1
re/spect/ful/ly	3,4	re/cep/tion	3,4

NAME _____

Invite volunteers, in turn, to read each sentence aloud and to circle the words containing two syllables. Then challenge the children to tell which syllabication tip applies to each word and to divide each word into syllables. You may remind the children that one-syllable words cannot be divided into syllables.

Extension

Writing   Duplicate the following sentences or write them on the chalkboard.
1. *Bud plays his trombone for an hour each day.*
2. *I have an appointment with the dentist today.*
3. *We saw many children at the circus.*
4. *Dry your wet mittens near the fireplace.*
5. *There were pretty balloons at the party.*

Direct the child to find and underline the words that conform to Syllabication Tip 5.

To extend the activity, ask the child to rewrite the underlined words, adding a slash to designate the syllables.

Recognition of Syllables   107

Divide the words below into syllables by drawing a slash between the syllables, as in the example. Some words may have one syllable.

1. nar/row/est	2. sun/set	3. un/grate/ful	4. gob/lin
5. ser/pents	6. lon/ger	7. moun/tain	8. un/com/mon
9. please	10. a/dop/tion	11. ac/cep/ted	12. mis/giv/ing
13. cen/sus	14. hol/low/ness	15. un/der/line	16. chap/ter
17. re/mem/ber	18. re/ad/just/ed	19. pic/nick/ing	20. cir/cus
21. per/fect/ly	22. com/bine	23. turn/pike	24. bet/ter
25. de/scribe	26. best	27. dis/ap/pear	28. cel/lo/phane
29. sand/wich/es	30. mis/spell	31. con/sis/tent/ly	32. un/cer/tain

Read the words that are part of each sentence. Finish the sentence by writing the words from the box in the correct order.

1. Faster driving is permitted on turnpikes but _____ not on city streets	not city on streets
2. Please ask questions if you do not understand the lesson perfectly	lesson understand the perfectly
3. Picnicking has been banned in the state park during the dry weather	dry the weather during
4. One person in the class will describe an object, and guessing the object will make a good game	a game good make
5. Rose is a better all-around athlete than Ellen, but Ellen is better at swimming	better is swimming at
6. David said, "I think the best act in the circus is the trapeze act	act is trapeze the
7. The entrance to the cave was found to be narrow	be to narrow found

NAME _____

Lesson 52
Recognition of Syllables (pages 108–110)

Objective   The child will apply Syllabication Tips 1 through 7 to divide words into syllables.

Syllabication Tip 6: When a single consonant comes between two vowels in a word, the word is usually divided after the consonant if the first vowel has a short sound. (cam/el)

Syllabication Tip 7: When a single consonant comes between two vowels in a word, the word is usually divided before the consonant if the first vowel has a long vowel sound. (tu/lip)

Review

Listening   To give children practice in identifying the number of syllables in a word, write the following words on the chalkboard and ask the children to tap out the syllables in each: curtain, picture, disown, dream, defrosting. Encourage volunteers to read the words aloud and to draw a slash between the syllables. If you wish, challenge the children to point out the syllabication tip that applies to each word.

Teaching Ideas

Listening   Write Syllabication Tip 6 on the chalkboard and ask a volunteer to read it aloud. Then list the following words on the chalkboard: cabin, tepid, palace, pedal, tonic, panic, river, finish, salad, wagon, camel. Encourage the children to read the words aloud and apply Syllabication Tip 6 to help them divide the words into syllables. Keep the tips on the chalkboard for the following lesson.

Write Syllabication Tip 7 on the chalkboard, and repeat the procedure using the following words: pecan, duty, radar, soda, motel, robot, lilac, music, bacon, meter. Keep the tips on the chalkboard for the following lesson.

Syllabication Game   Divide the class into two teams. Have members from each team come to the chalkboard. Direct each child at the chalkboard to listen to a word you say, write it on the chalkboard, and apply the syllabication tips to divide the word into syllables. Suggest that the children use slashes when dividing the word. Award two points to a team when a word is correctly spelled and divided into syllables. (You may award one point if only one of these tasks is correctly achieved.) Continue the game until each child has had a turn at the chalkboard. You may want to use the following words: slower, matchbox, return, wagon, pencil, tulip, restless, airport, misprint, seven, tiger, pillow.

---

108 Recognition of Syllables

Tip 6: When a single consonant comes between two vowels in a word, the word is usually divided after the consonant if the first vowel has a short sound. (cam/el)

Tip 7: When a single consonant comes between two vowels in a word, the word is usually divided before the consonant if the first vowel has a long sound. (tu/lip)

Say the name of the picture in each box. Then look at the word. Notice whether the first vowel has a long or short sound when a single consonant comes between two vowels. Use any tips that you know to divide the words into syllables. Write the syllables on the lines.

1. wagon — wag on	2. meter — me ter		
3. tiger — ti ger	4. peanut — pea nut		
5. beaver — bea ver	6. cabin — cab in		
7. seven — sev en	8. spider — spi der		
9. tomato — to ma to	10. robot — ro bot		
11. lemon — lem on	12. volcano — vol ca no		
13. blossom — blos som	14. giraffe — gir affe		
15. dragon — drag on	16. shadow — shad ow		
17. newspaper — news pa per	18. propeller — pro pel ler		
19. valentine — val en tine	20. groceries — gro cer ies		

NAME _____

---

109 Recognition of Syllables

Divide the following words into syllables, drawing a slash between each syllable. Write the number 6 or 7 after each word to show which tip you used.

duty	robot	lilac	tulip
river	camel	metal	pedal
melon	meter	zero	second
timid	polite	begin	label
never	secret	minus	pecan
habit	punish	damage	stupid
travel	denim	magic	nature

du/ty	7	li/lac	7
riv/er	6	met/al	6
mel/on	6	ze/ro	7
tim/id	6	be/gin	7
nev/er	6	mi/nus	7
hab/it	6	dam/age	6
trav/el	6	mag/ic	6
ro/bot	7	tu/lip	7
cam/el	6	ped/al	6
me/ter	7	sec/ond	6
po/lite	7	la/bel	7
se/cret	7	pe/can	7
pun/ish	6	stu/pid	7
den/im	6	na/ture	7

NAME _____

Reteaching

Listening   Say the following words one at a time: *abdominal, academic, barbershop, bedding, deck, cannon, enjoyment, reputation.* Encourage the child to tap for each syllable and then to tell you how many syllables are in each word.

Extension

Listening   Write the following words on the chalkboard.

duty	*departed*	*pedal*	*mimic*
lumber	*grapes*	*lemon*	*hopeful*
nighttime	*extend*	*thankful*	*daylight*
melon	*siren*	*airport*	*final*
planted	*tulip*	*cheerful*	*careless*

Direct the child to read each word, tap out the syllables, and indicate how many syllables the word has.

To expand the activity, ask the child to refer to the syllabication tips and to divide the words into syllables. Suggest that the child rewrite each word, placing a slash between the syllables.

Lesson 53
Recognition of Syllables (page 111)

Objective   The child will apply Syllabication Tips 1 through 8 to divide words into syllables.

Syllabication Tip 8: When a vowel is sounded alone in a word, it forms a syllable in itself. (*e/ven*)

Review

Speaking   To give the children practice dividing words into syllables, write the following words on the chalkboard and invite volunteers to draw slashes between the syllables in each word: *defrost, rain, priceless, duty, necklace, suffer, timid, matchbox.* Encourage the children to say each word aloud and to tell how many syllables the word has. Have the children refer to the syllabication tips on the chalkboard as they identify the tip that applies to each word.

Teaching Ideas

Reading   Say the following words aloud as you write them on the chalkboard: *unequal, unite, apron, comedy, equal, agree, president, element.* Encourage the children to identify the number of syllables in each word. Invite volun-

teers to draw slashes to indicate the syllable breaks in each word on the chalkboard. You might assign one child to verify the syllabication decisions for each word by referring to the dictionary. Revise syllabication errors according to the child's report. Then point out that in each of these words, a vowel forms a syllable in itself. Write Syllabication Tip 8 on the chalkboard and have a volunteer read it aloud. Keep Syllabication Tips 1 through 8 on the chalkboard.

Syllabication Game   Play the Syllabication Game described in Lesson 52 in this unit, and include the following words: *usual, spider, cozy, idea, motor, acorn, April, benefit, telegraph, polite.*

Reteaching

Writing   Write the following sentences on the chalkboard. Encourage the child to use Syllabication Tip 8 to help divide the underlined words.

1. Betty is a nickname for Elizabeth.
2. Ginger likes to ride an elevator.
3. Ten and one equal eleven.
4. My friend brought me a hat from Mexico.
5. The nurse is wearing a white uniform.

Extension

Writing   Duplicate the following sentences and challenge the child to underline those words that conform to Syllabication Tip 8.

1. Two and four are even numbers.
2. Dad wears an apron when he grills chicken.
3. Open the door with this key.
4. An acorn can grow into an oak tree.
5. The violin is a string instrument.
6. Todd watches television when his schoolwork is completed.

Recognition of Syllables   111

Tip 8: When a vowel is sounded alone in a word, it forms a syllable in itself. (e/ven)

Divide the words below into syllables, drawing a slash between each syllable.

unequal	gelatin	monument	telegraph
alarm	elephant	chemical	uniform
animals	telephone	adore	comedy
eleven	monitor	catalog	capital
benefit	ahead	cabinet	alibi
magazine	celebrate	delegate	depositor

un/e/qual	mon/u/ment
a/larm	chem/i/cal
an/i/mals	a/dore
e/lev/en	cat/a/log
ben/e/fit	cab/i/net
mag/a/zine	del/e/gate
gel/a/tin	tel/e/graph
el/e/phant	u/ni/form
tel/e/phone	com/e/dy
mon/i/tor	cap/i/tal
a/head	al/i/bi
cel/e/brate	de/pos/i/tor

NAME _____

80

Lesson 54
Recognition of Syllables (pages 112–113)

Objective The child will apply Syllabication Tips 1 through 9 to divide words into syllables.

Syllabication Tip 9: When two vowels found together in a word are pronounced separately, divide the word between the two vowels. (*po/em*)

Review

Reading To help the children recall Syllabication Tips 2 and 5, present the following word cards and ask the children to write the words with slashes between the syllables: *hornet, zipper, bathtub, thirteen, chairman*. Encourage the children to tell which tip applies to each word.

Teaching Ideas

Listening/Writing Say the following words one at a time, and ask the children to tell how many syllables are heard in each: *dial, giant, actual, siesta, tapioca, Ohio, manual*. Then, write these words on the chalkboard. Encourage the children to read the words aloud and to suggest how each word might be divided.

Reading Write Syllabication Tip 8 on the chalkboard under the other seven tips and ask a volunteer to read it aloud. Then ask the children to apply Syllabication Tip 8 to the underlined words in the following sentences.

1. Diana is very creative with her hands.
2. Violets and peonies are my favorite flowers.
3. Digging in a garden is tedious work.
4. The artist put her idea on canvas.
5. Robin prefers to listen to the radio.

(You might continue this activity by having the children identify the other multi-syllabic words in these sentences. Have the children apply the other tips to determine the breaks in syllables.)

Extension

Writing Display the following picture flashcards on the chalkboard ledge: *balloon, basket, book, lion, camel, doughnuts, jack-in-the-box, violin, newspaper, umbrella, box*. Direct the child to write the name for each picture on a sheet of paper. Encourage the child to sound the syllables in each word and to write the number next to the word. If you wish, challenge the child to divide the words using Syllabication Tips 1 through 8. Suggest that the child divide the words by rewriting them with slashes between each syllable. Keep the tips on the chalkboard for the next lesson.

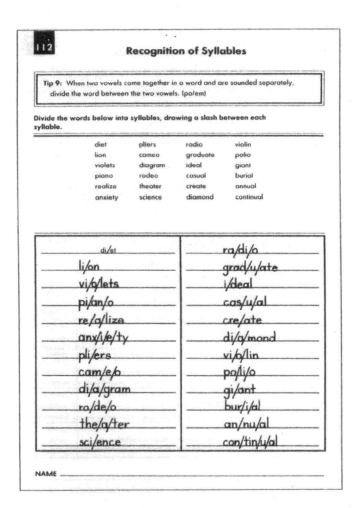

81

Lesson 55
Recognition of Syllables (pages 114–115)

Objective The child will apply Syllabication Tips 1 through 10 to divide words into syllables.

Syllabication Tip 10: When a word ends in *ckle*, divide the word between the *k* and the *le*. When a word ending in *le* is preceded by any other consonant, divide the word before that consonant. (*pick/le, bub/ble*)

Review

Speaking To give children practice in applying Syllabication Tips 5 and 6, write the following words on the chalkboard and have the children divide each word into syllables: *after, camel, seven, napkin, bitter, carpet, lemon, wagon, confide.* Encourage the children to read and to explain the tip that applies to each word.

Teaching Ideas

Reading Write Syllabication Tip 9 on the chalkboard, and invite a volunteer to read it aloud. Then, write the following words on the chalkboard, and ask the children to read each word aloud: *stable, fumble, table, little, middle,*

marble, tumble, purple, sparkle. Encourage volunteers to underline the last syllable in each word and give its sound. Invite the children to divide the words on the chalkboard into syllables, using Syllabication Tip 9 as a guide. Keep the tips on the chalkboard for the following lesson.

For additional practice, write the following words on the chalkboard, asking the children to pronounce each word and to divide it into syllables: *apple, middle, shingle, simple, angle, wrinkle, crumble, single, ankle.*

Extension

Writing Write the following sentences on the chalkboard. Leave space for writing above each sentence.
1. *Mary and Martha will play a duet with their fiddles.*
2. *Put the box of cereal in the middle of the table.*
3. *Leo wanted another helping of buttered noodles.*
4. *Runner number eleven is still ahead.*
5. *Sunday would be an ideal day for a picnic.*

Encourage the child to read the sentences and divide the underlined words into syllables. If you wish, challenge the child to write above each underlined word the number of the syllabication tip that applies.

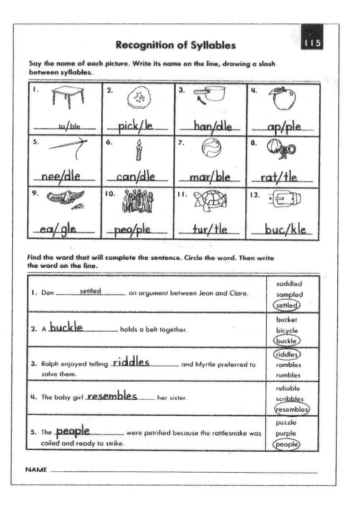

Lesson 56
Recognition of Syllables (pages 116–117)

Objective   The child will apply Syllabication Tips 1 through 10 to divide words into syllables.

Review

Reading   To reinforce the definition of a syllable, write the following words on the chalkboard and encourage the children to study them: *ankle, explain, tulip, earthquake, princess, alarm, faithful, shadow, rodeo.* Draw three lines under each word. Invite a volunteer to read the first word aloud. Then encourage that child to write the number of vowel sounds heard in the word on the first line under the word. Invite another child to write the number of vowels they see in the word on the second line. Ask a third child to write the number of syllables in the word on the third line. Continue the activity in this manner with each of the other words on the chalkboard.

Teaching Ideas

Reading   Write the following words on the chalkboard: *radiator, rattlesnake, examination, disrespectful.* Encourage the children to read the words aloud. Ask volunteers to suggest the syllable breaks in each word based on the syllabication tips. Encourage the volunteers to verify their suggestions by checking the syllabication in the dictionary.

Extension

Reading   Encourage the child to choose a short paragraph from a textbook or library book and to copy that paragraph onto a sheet of paper. Challenge the child to apply Syllabication Tips 1 through 10 to divide each word in the paragraph.

---

116   Recognition of Syllables

Read each tip. Use the tip to divide the words below it into syllables.
Draw a slash between each syllable.

Tip 1:   A one-syllable word is never divided.

     pass   thick   grapes   plant

Tip 2:   Divide a compound word between the words that form the compound word.

     foot/ball   flag/pole   earth/quake   stair/way

Tip 3:   When a word has a suffix, divide the word between the base word and the suffix if the suffix has a vowel sound.

     pain/ed   wish/ing   leaf/less   neat/ness

Tip 4:   When a word has a prefix, divide the word between the prefix and the base word.

     dis/pute   un/fair   de/frost   ex/plain

Tip 5:   When two or more consonants come between two vowels in a word, the word is usually divided between the first two consonants. Do not split blends or digraphs.

     prin/cess   bal/loon   sur/prise   pret/zel

Tip 6:   When a single consonant comes between two vowels in a word, the word is usually divided after the consonant if the first vowel has a short sound.

     wag/on   cam/el   shad/ow   sev/en

Tip 7:   When a single consonant comes between two vowels in a word, the word is usually divided before the consonant if the first vowel has a long sound.

     tu/lip   bea/ver   lo/cate   spi/der

Tip 8:   When a vowel is sounded alone in a word, it forms a syllable in itself.

     e/ven   u/ni/form   a/larm   cab/i/net

Tip 9:   When two vowels come together in a word and are sounded separately, divide the word between the vowels.

     po/em   ra/di/o   cre/ate   pi/an/o

Tip 10:   When a word ends in ckle, divide the word between the k and the le. When a word ending in le is preceded by any other consonant, divide the word before that consonant.

     pick/le   ea/gle   buck/le   star/tle

NAME _____

---

117   Recognition of Syllables

Divide the words below into syllables by drawing a slash between the syllables, as in the example. Some words have one syllable.

1. glass/es	2. dream/ing	3. thick/en	4. quick/ly
5. loud/er	6. neat/ness	7. con/clu/sion	8. point/ed
9. or/ches/tra	10. en/joy/able	11. land/ed	12. box/es
13. cen/sus	14. lunch/es	15. chim/pan/zee	16. tri/umph
17. thank/ful	18. proud/ly	19. dis/re/spect/ful	20. de/part/ing
21. truck/ed	22. con/nec/tion	23. birds	24. short/est
25. air/plane	26. ex/ten/sion	27. par/o/graph	28. hy/phen
29. screw/driv/er	30. weak/en	31. squint/ing	32. brush/es
33. weights	34. mois/ten	35. taste/less	36. like/ness
37. a/gree/able	38. un/pun/ished	39. strength/en	40. ex/am/i/na/tion
41. ex/cur/sion	42. mis/con/cep/tion	43. pres/i/dent	44. musk/mel/on
45. de/part/ed	46. rat/tle/snake	47. dis/ap/pear	48. hel/i/cop/ter

Read the words that are part of each sentence. Finish the sentence by writing the words from the box in the correct order.

1. Bob has a pet chimpanzee	mimics exactly that him
2. Janet's chances of dicovering gold are very remote	very gold remote are
3. We flew in a helicopter at a low altitude	low a at altitude
4. When you divide words into syllables, use hyphens between the syllables	syllables between hyphens the
5. Ray delivered a load of packages to the post office yesterday	office yesterday post the

NAME _____

83

Lesson 57
Adding Suffixes (pages 118–120)

Objective The child will apply spelling tips to add suffixes *es*, *ed*, *ing*, *er*, and *est* to words.

When a word ends in *Y* preceded by a consonant, change the *Y* to *I* before adding a suffix other than *ing*.

When a word ends in silent *e*, drop the *e* from the base word before adding *ed* or *ing*.

When a short vowel word ends in a single consonant, the consonant is usually doubled before adding the suffix.

Review

Speaking To reinforce the children's understanding of suffixes, encourage them to explain how suffixes change the meanings of various base words. Write the following words in columns on the chalkboard: *bug, bugs; tan, tanned; dream, dreaming; big, bigger, biggest*. Encourage the children to define the base words and then to tell the meaning of each base word when the suffix is added.

Teaching Ideas

Spelling Write the following key words in a row on the chalkboard, and encourage the children to read them aloud: *play, fry, carry*. Point out the final *y* in each word. Ask a volunteer to identify the letter before the final *y* in *play*. Point out that the letter *Y* is a vowel. Then write the following words underneath the key word: *plays, played*. Stress that the base word does not change when a suffix is added to a word that ends with a vowel plus *Y*. Then ask a volunteer to identify the letters before the final *y* in *fly* and *carry*. Point out that these letters are consonants. Explain the first spelling tip for this letter and write the following words under the key word *cry*: *cries, cried*. Encourage the children to spell the words aloud with you. Repeat the spelling tip for the children, and ask them to apply it to the third key word, *carry*. Then ask the children to apply the spelling tip to each of the following words: *supplies, spies, hurries, fried, tried*.

Write the following key words in a row on the chalkboard, and ask the children to identify the final vowel in each. Read the second spelling tip to the children, and encourage them to add the suffixes *ed* and *ing* to each of the key words.

Read the third spelling tip to the children and then write the following key words in a row on the chalkboard: *stop, beg, trim, rub*. Point out the short vowel sound in each word. Then

---

Adding Suffixes

When a word that ends in y is preceded by a consonant, change the y to i before adding a suffix other than ing.

Add the suffixes **es** and **ed** to each base word below.

cry	1.	cries	2.	cried
spy	3.	spies	4.	spied
dry	5.	dries	6.	dried
try	7.	tries	8.	tried
deny	9.	denies	10.	denied
copy	11.	copies	12.	copied
hurry	13.	hurries	14.	hurried

When a word ends with a silent e, we usually drop the e from the base word before adding ed or ing.

Add the suffixes **ed** and **ing** to each base word below.

use	1.	used	2.	using
bake	3.	baked	4.	baking
like	5.	liked	6.	liking
vote	7.	voted	8.	voting
save	9.	saved	10.	saving
share	11.	shared	12.	sharing
wipe	13.	wiped	14.	wiping

NAME _____

Adding Suffixes

When a short vowel word ends in a single consonant, we usually double the consonant before adding the suffix.

Add the suffixes **ed** and **ing** to each base word below.

can	1.	canned	2.	canning
dim	3.	dimmed	4.	dimming
sun	5.	sunned	6.	sunning
beg	7.	begged	8.	begging
kiss	9.	kissed	10.	kissing
trim	11.	trimmed	12.	trimming
clap	13.	clapped	14.	clapping

Using the three tips for adding suffixes, add **er** and **est** to each base word below.

safe	1.	safer	2.	safest
sad	3.	sadder	4.	saddest
thin	5.	thinner	6.	thinnest
funny	7.	funnier	8.	funniest
brave	9.	braver	10.	bravest
long	11.	longer	12.	longest
happy	13.	happier	14.	happiest
slow	15.	slower	16.	slowest

NAME _____

---

provide an example by writing *stopped* and *stopping* under the key word *stop*. Encourage the children to add the suffixes *ed* and *ing* to the other key words on the chalkboard.

Suffix Game   Stack cards containing suffixes facedown on the desk. Then write the following words in two columns on the chalkboard: *cry, copy, bake, study, wipe, paste, care, love; brave, safe, thin, funny, long, happy, hot, hum.* Invite the children to choose a suffix from the stack and to identify it for the other children. If the child has the suffix *ed, es,* or *ing,* challenge the child to add the suffix to a word in the first column. If the child has the suffix *er* or *est,* challenge the child to add the suffix to a word in the second column. Continue until the children have added a suffix to each word listed on the chalkboard. To vary the game, divide the class into teams and award points for each correct answer.

Extension

Writing   Direct the child to apply the spelling tips to add *er* and *est* to the following words: *happy, safe, sad, funny, wise, big.*

| 120 | **Adding Suffixes** |

Read the words that are part of each sentence. Finish the sentence by adding a suffix to the base word in the box. Write the new word on the line.

1. On a long hike, the last mile is the ___hardest___	hard
2. Shopping is lots of fun for some people, but **boring** for others.	bore
3. Jill and her classmates **decorated** the classroom for the meeting last night.	decorate
4. Ronald **hummed** a tune while he was riding his bicycle.	hum
5. It is a good idea to get used to **sharing** with others.	share
6. There is no use **denying** that you will feel bad if you do not get a part in the class play.	deny
7. The old road into town is **shorter** than the new highway.	short
8. Today is the **hottest** day so far this year.	hot
9. Theresa was the **bravest** girl at camp. She saved one of the other campers from drowning.	brave
10. It is too warm outside to wear that shirt, so wear a **thinner** one.	thin
11. The children roared when the clown performed his **funniest** trick.	funny

NAME _____

Lesson 58
Contractions (pages 121–122)

Objective The child will form and read contractions appearing in isolation and in sentences.

Review

Reading To give children practice in identifying syllables, encourage the children to read the following words, divide them into syllables, and explain the syllabication tip that applies: *thick, startle, camel, flagpole, unfair, balloon, create, thankful.*

Teaching Ideas

Speaking Write the following phrases and contractions in three rows on the chalkboard: *I am, I'm; let us, let's; did not, didn't.* Then write the word *contraction* and remind the children that a contraction is a shortened phrase in which one or more letters have been omitted. Encourage the children to read the phrase and contraction in each row and tell which letters have been omitted to make the contraction. Circle the apostrophes and explain that the apostrophe in a contraction takes the place of the missing letters.

Present the following word cards: *he will, are not, do not, he is, they are, I have.* Ask the children to read each phrase, state the appropriate contraction for the phrase, and spell the contraction.

Writing Write the following sentences on the chalkboard.
1. *Let us go swimming today.*
2. *We have gone to that park before.*
3. *How did you know that I am surprised?*
4. *Mom does not want to mow the lawn.*
5. *We will call before we come to visit.*

Encourage the children to read the sentences aloud, replace the underlined phrases with the appropriate contractions, and then reread the sentences.

Extension

Writing Write the following phrases on the chalkboard: *I have, have not, would not, there is, she will, you are.* Direct the child to write the appropriate contraction for each phrase and then to write a sentence using the contraction.

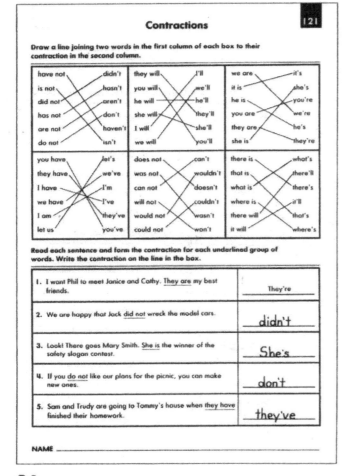

Unit 16 Synonyms, Antonyms, and Homonyms

Lesson 59

Synonyms   (page 123)

Objective   The child will identify and read words that are synonyms.

Review

Speaking   To reinforce the children's vocabulary, list the following words on the chalkboard, and ask the children to define each word: *rapidly, gladly, bashful, breakable*. Challenge the children to use these words to complete the sentences you will say. Then read the following incomplete sentences to the children.

1. *Jim speaks softly because he is _____ .*
2. *Be careful with that _____ vase.*
3. *I will _____ pay you Thursday.*
4. *She jumped _____ out of the dog's path.*

Teaching Ideas

Speaking   Write the following words on the chalkboard and ask the children to name a word that means the same or almost the same as the given word: *large, little, shut, quick, tidy, poky*. Write the children's responses on the chalkboard. Then pronounce the word *synonym* and write it on the chalk-board. Explain to the children that words meaning the same thing are called *synonyms*. Write the word *same* on the chalkboard under the word *synonym*, and circle the beginning *s* in each word. Point out that both words begin with the letter *s*. Encourage the children to use the common letter to help them recall the meaning of the word *synonym*.

Synonym Game   Divide the class into two teams. You might prepare the following word cards and give each child on the first team a card: *moist, stay, repeat, trail, display, easy*. Give each child in the second team a word card that has a similar meaning: *damp, remain, retell, follow, show, simple*. Encourage the children on each team to seek out the partner holding the synonym for the word each has. When the partners have found each other, ask them to write their words on the chalkboard.

To expand the game, challenge the partner to write a sentence for each of the words.

Reteaching

Writing   Write the following words on the chalk-board: *difficult, correct, errors, simple*. Ask the child to suggest a synonym for each word and then to use the synonym in a sentence.

87

Lesson 60
Antonyms (pages 124–125)

Objective The child will identify and read words that are antonyms.

Review To recall the meanings of the prefixes *mis* and *un*, write the following words on the chalkboard, asking the children to define each: *mislead, misspell, mispronounce, unfair, unkind, unwind, unbuckle*. Encourage volunteers to circle the prefix of each word and to tell what each word means.

Teaching Ideas

Speaking Write the following words on the chalkboard and ask the children to name a word that means the opposite of each word: *sweet, laugh, up, left, quiet, good, buy, in*. Write the children's responses on the chalkboard. Then pronounce the word *antonym* and write it on the chalkboard. Explain to the children that words with opposite meanings are called *antonyms*.

Writing Write the following words in a row at the top of the chalkboard: *short, weak, sunny, wide, go, new*. Then write the following sentences on the chalkboard, underlining words as indicated.

1. *Roy is a tall man.*
2. *Will has very strong arm muscles.*
3. *Today is a cloudy day.*
4. *Please come home for lunch today.*
5. *I am wearing my old shoes.*
6. *This river is quite narrow.*

Encourage the children to read each sentence and then to substitute an antonym on the chalkboard for the underlined word.

Reteaching

Matching Write the following words in columns as shown.

Synonyms		Antonyms	
strange	petite	disagree	dirty
silent	luggage	inside	outside
tiny	quiet	clean	rise
baggage	odd	fall	agree

Ask the child to give the meaning of each heading. Then direct the child to match the words in both columns under each heading. You may want to complete the first match for the child.

---

124 Antonyms

Draw a line joining the words that have the opposite meaning.

pretty	noisy	full	cold	hard	dirty
dull	slow	warm	cool	asleep	soft
quiet	ugly	hot	well	strong	fearless
useful	bright	sick	empty	clean	weak
fast	useless	smile	frown	fearful	awake
inside	return	level	stop	first	last
tall	lower	painless	short	fall	helpful
raise	short	long	forbid	helpless	unspoken
climb	descend	allow	uneven	spoken	small
leave	outside	start	painful	large	rise
purchase	sadness	sweet	like	join	disagree
gladness	sell	wise	export	cause	deflate
longest	untidy	hate	lie	agree	separate
neat	inaction	truth	sour	for	prevent
action	shortest	import	foolish	inflate	near

Finish each sentence by adding an antonym for the word in the box. Write the antonym on the line.

1. Joan, it is time to turn the light ___off___ and go to sleep.	on
2. Bill, you will find your socks ___under___ your chair.	over
3. These bakery rolls taste good because they are nice and ___fresh___.	stale
4. Carlos, do you dream a lot when you are ___asleep___?	awake
5. Jenny spread a ___thick___ layer of peanut butter on her bread.	thin

NAME _____

---

125 Synonyms and Antonyms

Read the pair of words in each box. Write an A if the words are antonyms. Write an S if the words are synonyms.

1. pretty ugly — A	2. moist damp — S	3. empty full — A
4. trail follow — S	5. enlarge expand — S	6. truth falsehood — A
7. cause prevent — A	8. longest shortest — A	9. stay remain — S
10. allow forbid — A	11. complete finish — S	12. wise foolish — A
13. unusual uncommon — S	14. join separate — A	15. unshaven bearded — S

Read the words that are part of each sentence. Finish the sentence by writing the words from the box in the correct order.

1. Bill's room is always neat, while his sister's ___room is always untidy___	is room always untidy
2. The balloon deflated overnight, so we will ___have to reinflate it___	to it reinflate have
3. Our cat Tab, climbed a tall oak tree, but it was ___afraid to descend it___	afraid it descend to
4. Dad is going to sell his old car and ___purchase a new one___	one new purchase a
5. It is usually so noisy here that ___the quietness seems strange___	strange quietness the seems

NAME _____

Lesson 61
Homonyms (pages 126–128)

Objective The child will identify and read homonyms appearing in isolation and in sentences.

Review

To reinforce the children's understanding of synonyms and antonyms, write the following pairs of words on the chalkboard: *pretty/ugly, wise/foolish, import/export, complete/finish, cause/prevent.* Encourage the children to read the word pairs aloud, define the words in each pair, and tell whether the words are synonyms or antonyms.

Teaching Ideas

Listening Write the following word pairs in columns on the chalkboard and ask the children to read the words aloud: *sail/sale, buy/by, see/sea.* Then pronounce the word *homonym,* and write it on the chalkboard. Tell the children that homonyms are words that sound alike but are spelled differently and mean different things. Encourage the children to reread the homonyms above and to use each word in a sentence.

Speaking Present the following word cards and ask the children to say and spell a homonym for each: *blue, hear, knows, meet, sent, steel, weak.* As the children respond cor-

rectly, write each pair of homonyms on the chalkboard. To check the children's comprehension of the homonyms, ask them to create a sentence for each pair of words.

Continue the activity by asking the children to say and spell homonyms for the following words: *rode, pale, to, there, main.*

Direct the children to listen carefully as you read the following sentences aloud, one at a time.

1. *We knew he would buy a new car.*
2. *I like hot soup and warm bread for lunch.*
3. *We won one of the awards at the band concert.*
4. *They begin practice at four o'clock and finish at six o'clock.*

Pause after reading each sentence, and invite a volunteer to tell whether the sentence contains two synonyms, two antonyms, or two homonyms. Encourage the children to identify the two words and write them on the chalkboard. Direct the children to write the letter *S, A,* or *H* next to the words to identify the words as synonyms, antonyms, or homonyms.

Writing Write the following words in a row at the top of the chalkboard: *by, sent, red, buy, write, cent, read, right.* Then write the following incomplete sentences on the chalkboard.

1. *She went to the store to _____ apples.*
2. *Carlos _____ his letter yesterday.*
3. *I _____ a book about dogs.*
4. *Sue-Lin doesn't like to _____ letters.*

Encourage the children to read the sentences and to fill in the blanks with words listed on the chalkboard. Invite volunteers to read the completed sentences aloud.

Extension

Listening   Say the following pairs of words and have the child identify the members of each pair as synonyms, antonyms, or homonyms.

start/begin	*summer/winter*	*eight/ate*
lift/raise	*happen/occur*	*quick/fast*
late/early	*would/wood*	*high/low*
stair/stare	*brake/break*	*lose/win*

Family Involvement Activity   Duplicate the Family Letter on page 96 of this Teacher's Edition. Send it home with the children.

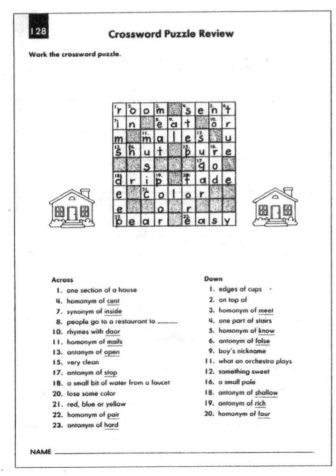

128   **Crossword Puzzle Review**

Work the crossword puzzle.

Across
1. one section of a house
4. homonym of cent
7. synonym of inside
8. people go to a restaurant to _____
10. rhymes with door
11. homonym of mails
13. antonym of open
15. very clean
17. antonym of stop
18. a small bit of water from a faucet
20. lose some color
21. red, blue or yellow
22. homonym of pair
23. antonym of hard

Down
1. edges of cups
2. on top of
3. homonym of meat
4. one part of stairs
5. homonym of know
6. antonym of false
9. boy's nickname
11. what an orchestra plays
12. something sweet
16. a small pole
18. antonym of shallow
19. antonym of rich
20. homonym of four

NAME _____

90

Date: _____

A Note to the Family—

We are using PHONICS IS FUN in your child's class. The skills taught in the program will help your child become a better reader. I will send a Family Involvement Activity home with your child for most phonics units. These activities are similar to those your child _____ does in school. Your participation in these activities will help your child develop and review the skills learned in the classroom.

The following Family Involvement Activity reviews the skills covered in Unit Three. This activity involves little preparation, and the materials are common household items. For the Unit Three activity, your child will write riddles for compound words that have the short vowel sounds of *a, e, i, o,* and *u.* (Your child will know that a *compound word* is a word that is made up of two or more words, such as *uphill.*)

Encourage your child to learn the following riddles and to ask family members and friends to answer them.

1. *What do you use to carry your camping equipment around? (backpack)*
2. *What is a device with long arms that turn in the wind? (windmill)*
3. *What do you call the place in an airplane where the pilot and the crew sit? (cockpit)*
4. *What do you call the pretty colors you see in the sky at the end of the day? (sunset)*

Challenge your child to create additional riddles for compound words with short vowels. Direct your child to write the riddle on the front of a card or sheet of paper, and the answer on the back. You might encourage your child to include clues telling the short vowel sounds used in each word, such as, *What is the place where you get clean each evening? It has the short sound of* a *and the short sound of* u*? (bathtub)*

Please encourage your child to complete the riddles at home with your family's assistance. Completed projects may be returned to the classroom by (date) _____ and will become part of our classroom display.

Thank you for your cooperation. Your comments are always welcome.

Sincerely,

Comments: _____

_____

_____

_____

_____

Date: _____

A Note to the Family—

We are using PHONICS IS FUN in your child's class. The skills taught in the program will help your child become a better reader. I will send a Family Involvement Activity home with your child for most phonics units. These activities are similar to those your child _____ does in school. Your participation in these activities will help your child develop and review the skills learned in the classroom.

The following Family Involvement Activity reviews the skills covered in Unit Four. This activity involves little preparation, and the materials are common household items. For the Unit Four activity, your child will write words with the long sounds of the vowels *a, e, i, o,* and *u*.

Help your child prepare a catalog of long vowel words by taking six sheets of blank paper and stapling them together on one side. Suggest the title, *LONG VOWEL CATALOG*, and help your child to write these words on the cover page. Invite your child to copy the following headings on the inside pages of the booklet: *Long a, Long e, Long i, Long o, Long u.* Encourage your child to cut pictures of objects with names that contain long vowel sounds from old catalogs and magazines. Have your child paste each picture on the page beneath the appropriate heading. You might help your child write each picture name under the object. Suggest that your child imagine that each object is available for mail order. Encourage your child to list prices, sizes, and colors of the various objects.

Please encourage your child to complete the catalog at home with your family's assistance. Completed projects may be returned to the classroom by (date)_____ and will become part of our classroom display.

Thank you for your cooperation. Your comments are always welcome.

Sincerely,

Comments: _____

_____

_____

_____

_____

Date: _____

A Note to the Family—

We are using PHONICS IS FUN in your child's class. The skills taught in the program will help your child become a better reader. I will send a Family Involvement Activity home with your child for most phonics units. These activities are similar to those your child _____ does in school. Your participation in these activities will help your child develop and review the skills learned in the classroom.

The following Family Involvement Activity reviews the skills covered in Unit Seven. This activity involves little preparation, and the materials are common household items. For the Unit Seven activity, your child will write riddles for words containing the vowels *y* and *w*, and for words containing the hard and soft sounds of *c* and *g*. (Use the following words as samples: hard *g/goat*, soft *g/gem*, hard *c/cat*, soft *c/city*.)

Encourage your child to write or to memorize the following riddles and to ask family members and friends to answer them.

1. *Name something with a hard* g *that you open and go through to pick your vegetables.* (garden gate)
2. *What words with* y *as a vowel describe a newborn dog that looks like a tiny fish?* (guppy puppy)
3. *Name a friendly group of cheese-eating rodents whose name has a soft* c. (nice mice)
4. *What name with* w *as a vowel could you use for a hair ribbon that is the color of the sun?* (yellow bow)
5. *What hard* c *words name a heavy piece of clothing to wear in your automobile?* (car coat)
6. *Name a very large animal with a long neck and a soft* g *in its name.* (huge giraffe)

Help your child create additional riddles for words containing vowels *y* and *w*, and words with the hard and soft sounds of *c* and *g*. Direct your child to write the riddle on the front of a card or sheet of paper and the answer on the back. Encourage your child to use two-word answers and suggest that your child provide clues to the number of syllables in each word.

Please encourage your child to complete the riddles at home with your family's assistance. Completed projects may be returned to the classroom by (date) _____ and will become part of our classroom display.

Thank you for your cooperation. Your comments are always welcome.

Sincerely,

Comments: _____

_____

_____

Date: _____

A Note to the Family—

We are using PHONICS IS FUN in your child's class. The skills taught in the program will help your child become a better reader. I will send a Family Involvement Activity home with your child for most phonics units. These activities are similar to those your child _____ does in school. Your participation in these activities will help your child develop and review the skills learned in the classroom.

The following Family Involvement Activity reviews the skills covered in Unit Twelve. This activity involves little preparation, and the materials are common household items. For the Unit Twelve activity, your child will combine base words, such as *branch* or *odd*, with suffixes, such as *es* or *er*.

Play a game of Word Card Challenge in which both players combine base words, such as *lunch*, with suffixes, such as *es*. Prepare the game materials by helping your child write each of the following base words and suffixes on index cards or squares of cardboard: *branch, fox, ask, buzz, lunch, egg, miss, tax, train, punch, laugh, small, soft, odd, fast, near, s, es, ed, er, est.* Separate the cards with base words from the cards with endings. Then shuffle both stacks and place them facedown on the table. Take turns selecting the top card from each stack. If the word card can be combined with the ending card to form a new word, the player writes the new word on a sheet of paper and returns the word card to the bottom of the stack. If the word and the ending cannot be combined, the player holds the word card until the next turn, when a new ending card is drawn. At the end of each turn, place the ending card at the bottom of the stack.

Please encourage your child to write each of the words created during the Word Card Challenge. Completed lists may be returned to the classroom by (date) _____ and will become part of our classroom display.

Thank you for your cooperation. Your comments are always welcome.

Sincerely,

Comments: _____
_____
_____
_____
_____

Date: _____

A Note to the Family—

We are using PHONICS IS FUN in your child's class. The skills taught in the program
will help your child become a better reader. I will send a Family Involvement Activity
home with your child for most phonics units. These activities are similar to those your
child _____ does in school. Your participation in these activities
will help your child develop and review the skills learned in the classroom.

The following Family Involvement Activity reviews the skills covered in Unit Thirteen.
This activity involves little preparation, and the materials are common household items.
For the Unit Thirteen activity, your child will combine base words, such as *like,* with
prefixes, such as *dis*.

Help your child read the prefixes and base words in the following chart.

Prefixes	Base Words		
un–	new	press	close
dis–	place	tell	turn
re–	charge	frost	safe
ex–	honest	charge	like
de–	lock	take	happy
mis–	rail	fair	pose
	trust	obey	fuse

Challenge your child to create as many real words as possible by combining the prefixes
with the base words. Encourage your child to use as many prefixes with each base word
as possible. If you wish, you can present the activity as a competitive game by setting a
time limit and challenging two players to write as many words as possible within the
given time limit.

Please encourage your child to list the new words with your family's assistance.
Completed lists may be returned to the classroom by (date)_____ and will
become part of our classroom display.

Thank you for your cooperation. Your comments are always welcome.

Sincerely,

Comments: _____

_____

_____

Date: _____

A Note to the Family—

We are using PHONICS IS FUN in your child's class. The skills taught in the program will help your child become a better reader. I will send a Family Involvement Activity home with your child for most phonics units. These activities are similar to those your child _____ does in school. Your participation in these activities will help your child develop and review the skills learned in the classroom.

The following Family Involvement Activity reviews the skills covered in Unit Sixteen. This activity involves little preparation, and the materials are common household items. For the Unit Sixteen activity, your child will identify word pairs as synonyms, antonyms, or homonyms. (Your child will know that *synonyms* have the same meanings, *antonyms* have opposite meanings, and *homonyms* sound the same but have different spellings and meanings.)

Play a synonym/antonym/homonym game with your child. Prepare the game materials by helping your child write the following headings in a row on a sheet of paper: *Synonyms, Antonyms,* and *Homonyms.* Then help your child write the following word pairs on index cards or small pieces of cardboard.

sad/happy	*inside/outside*	*cool/warm*	*nose/knows*
high/low	*ate/eight*	*big/large*	*well/healthy*
quiet/still	*rich/poor*	*simple/easy*	*break/brake*
maid/made	*die/dye*	*well/sick*	*friend/enemy*
protect/guard	*two/too*	*find/lose*	*not/knot*

Shuffle the word cards and divide them equally between you and your child. Then take turns flashing a word card to the other player who must tell whether the words are synonyms, antonyms, or homonyms. If the player answers correctly, have your child write the word pair under the correct heading. If the player answers incorrectly, let the challenger attempt an answer. The person with the most cards at the end of the game is the winner.

Please encourage your child to write the list of synonyms, antonyms, and homonyms. Completed lists may be returned to the classroom by (date) _____ and will become part of our classroom display.

Thank you for your cooperation. Your comments are always welcome.

Sincerely,

Comments: _____

_____

_____

_____

Phonics Is Fun
Index of Skills

	Lesson Numbers		
	Book 1	Book 2	Book 3
Antonyms		63	60
Compound words			
long vowel		23	14
short vowel		16	10
Consonants			
digraphs	66–68	29, 30, 58, 59	18, 19, 34, 35
hard and soft *c*		31	21, 23
hard and soft *g*		32	22, 23
l blends	63	25	16
letter-sound association	8–27	2–10	2–4
r blends	62	24	15
s blends	64	26	17
Contractions		46–49	58
Ending *le*		60	36
Homonyms		64	61
Prefixes		61	46–49
Recognition of letters	2–7	1	1
Suffixes	59–61	36–45	39–44, 57
Syllabication			37, 38, 45, 50–56
Synonyms		62	59
Two-syllable words		17, 23	10
Visual discrimination	1		
Vowels			
digraphs		50–53	27–30
diphthongs		54–57	31–33
long *a*	43–45	18	11
long *e*	55–57	22	13
long *i*	46–48	19	11
long *o*	52–54	21	12
long *u*	49–51	20	12
review of	58		
seen and heard			37
short *a*	28–30	11	5
short *e*	40–42	15	9
short *i*	31–33	12	6
short *o*	37–39	14	8
short *u*	34–36	13	7
w		28	20
with *r*		33–35	24–26
y	65	27	20

Made in the USA
Middletown, DE
14 July 2023

35153311R00055